Be Stylish

With

Pernia Qureshi

EBURY PRESS

An imprint of Penguin Random House

EBURY PRESS

USA | Canada | UK | Ireland | Australia
New Zealand | India | South Africa | China | Singapore

Ebury Press is part of the Penguin Random House group of companies whose addresses can be found at global.penguinrandomhouse.com

Published by Penguin Random House India Pvt. Ltd
4th Floor, Capital Tower 1, MG Road,
Gurugram 122 002, Haryana, India

Penguin
Random House
India

First Published by Random House India in 2013
This edition published in Ebury Press by Penguin Random House India 2021

10 9 8 7 6 5 4 3 2

ISBN 9788184003741

For sale in the Indian Subcontinent only

Typeset in ElegantGaramond BT by R. Ajith Kumar
Printed at Repro India Limited

www.penguin.co.in

FSC
www.fsc.org
MIX
Paper from responsible sources
FSC® C047271

'I'm jealous even of the wind that
blows through her hair'
—Delavga

For My Mom

CONTENTS

FOREWORD

The moment I met Pernia, we instantly connected over our undying love for all things fashion and style! We spent hours together, on movie sets and in our homes, comparing notes on the latest trends, our favourite designers and of course red carpet hits and misses. I discovered that we had the same sense of aesthetic and this is why I trust her blindly when it comes to dressing me.

Since *Aisha*, which is when we spent countless hours together in my office as I tried on hundreds of costumes, there has been no looking back for Pernia's career and our friendship. Since then, we always bounce off ideas, trading countless emails on what to wear next, whether at work or events and parties. It's such a blessing to have a sincere friend who gives an honest opinion, even in fashion emergencies.

And, our friendship has survived our differences! The one thing we always argue on is the amount of accessories I wear. I am constantly putting on as many as I can and she is constantly removing them. Pernia is a strong believer in minimalism. On that front we have amicably agreed to disagree.

Pernia is led by her passions and instinct. Her impeccable taste, strong sense of creativity, and immense drive has resulted in **Pernia's Pop-Up Shop**, which revolutionized how people shop in India. For the first time, she has made Indian designer wear easily accessible to style lovers from the remotest of towns around the country and to all the Indian fashionistas around the globe. I was one of the first customers and today it is my go-to store where I almost always find something to suit my mood. From the sets of *Aisha* to owning India's first luxury online boutique, Pernia has come a long way and I am extremely happy and proud to play some part in that journey.

This book is the perfect next step in Pernia's career. With her creative experience and deep understanding of the psyche of Indian women and their bodies, there is no better person to offer style advice than Pernia. I am elated to share her with everyone so India can become an even more stylish place, one woman at a time.

Use this book as your best kept secret and style bible. It can truly change the way you see yourself and give you the confidence to *Be Stylish* just like me.

Love

Sonam Kapoor
Mumbai, 2013

INTRODUCTION

I didn't study fashion or take any classes in style, but I guess you could say it's always been part of my embroidery.

My progression from an over-dressed toddler in a sari to a fully blown stylist with my own online boutique has been a journey of passion and imagination, as well as self-knowledge. It began around the same time I started Indian classical dance. Although I was just four, I absolutely adored wearing the outfits, jingling around in heavy jewellery. I remember spinning around on stage, seeing my skirt twirling in front of me and feeling so beautiful. This was the first time that I felt the transformative power of dressing.

Although I had attended many Indian shows in school, I didn't attend my first catwalk show outside India until after I had left college. It was the 2008 Chanel Spring couture show in Paris and the theme was 'arctic freeze'. I thought I knew what a catwalk show would involve, but nothing could prepare me for the tingling sensation I felt upon witnessing these hand-crafted, precious creations glide down the runway. I was enchanted; I forgot my career in law and instead anchored myself in the realm of clothing—a world where my burning passions and talents lay.

The last few years have been a total adventure, one where I never stopped learning. Since that tummy-flipping moment in Paris, I've worked for fashion magazines, on film sets, and even crafted my own clothing line. My career has transported me around the world and across dozens of seasonal trends.

BUT WHETHER I'M DRESSING A MOVIE CHARACTER LIKE AISHA OR A MODEL FOR A SHOOT, ONE FACT REMAINS THE SAME: THE OUTFIT MUST REFLECT THE INSIDE OF THE PERSON OR CHARACTER, OTHERWISE IT'S SIMPLY NOT STYLISH.

I have to understand the personality of whoever I'm dressing and only then can I style them accordingly. In this sense, I guess you could say I'm less of a stylist and more like a psychologist! Only without the white coat and the couch...

So what exactly denotes 'style' and how can my book help you to be 'stylish'?

If you're looking for Ten Commandments on how to categorize your wardrobe or a rule book which will guide you around Zara, then I'm afraid you'll need to strut on by.

In the chapters that follow, you'll find hundreds of hints and tips to help you dress stylishly, but this end purpose is only possible when you have learnt that there's only one room in my sartorial classroom:

Self Love

Best summed up in two words, three syllables—'Know Thyself'.

Go ahead, scrawl it on your mirror in lipstick, and we can begin.

STYLE COMES FROM WITHIN, IT EMANATES FROM AN UNDERSTANDING OF YOUR PAST PERSONALITY AND FUTURE AMBITIONS.

Being stylish is all about the confidence in streamlining this knowledge, in having the guts to present your inner self to the world with a beaming smile and a breezy flick of your hair.

Mediate the media—don't be a puppet on a string!

Too many women of all ages confuse style with fashion and trends. Here is the first myth that I want to debunk in my boxing ring. Pow! Round one. Out cold!

Saint Coco Chanel's statement about the changeability of fashion versus the timeless longevity of style is why this book focusses on the latter rather than the former. Here is where you all need to recognize the difference between my advice to you in the following chapters and what you might read in fashion magazines. While these magazines are beautiful in their own right and are compiled by some of the finest minds in the industry, you have to understand that the fashion world spins on a dizzying axis of trends and seasonal styles.

BEING STYLISH TODAY IS ABOUT BEING SENSITIVE TO, YET SENSIBLE OF, THE OFTEN BIZARRE AGENDAS OF DESIGNERS AND MAGAZINE EDITORS. ADHERE TOO CLOSELY TO THE TRENDS THEY PREACH AND YOU RISK COMPROMISING YOUR OWN UNIQUE AESTHETIC.

All stylish women and my favourite fashionistas know that, as tempting it can be to devour *Cosmo* for breakfast only to remerge by dinner-time clad in seasonally tuned-plum, pleat and peplum, this is not the right way to nurture your inner Vogue. One thing I hate about today's media is how intimidating fashion magazines can be! That's what sometimes prevents so many people from actually taking chances and fully expressing themselves, from having fun with fashion. Those who celebrate style will usually be found smiling and exhibiting a sense of humour in their dressing. Those who abide by strict rules of 'fashion' rarely smile and tend to pout only.

Pssst...take my advice, skip over those pages which tell you 'what not to wear', those features which list the dos and don'ts of fashion, or what to clear out of your closet. Keep it messy if you like it that way. All too often I read these articles, only to realize, oh my god, at this very moment, I'm wearing the same item they're telling me to chuck out! Luckily I have a thick skin, but I know how persuasive and inhibiting these rule-based articles can be, so stay away if you can.

What I absolutely adore in fashion magazines, and a feature that we include on my own website is Street Style. Another demi-God of style after Saint Coco Chanel would have to be Scott Schuman, a New York-based photographer who created satorialist.com, a website which snaps stylish men and women walking the streets all over the world, from Mumbai to Milan. Schuman is a genius because he documented the relationship between trends and daily life. He enabled us to pause that moment when we walk past someone who is dressed amazingly and savour their outfit a little longer. His website was one of the first fashion blogs to celebrate and champion individual style rather than universal trends. As a web resource, Street Style blogs are your best friends. Go ahead and google it!

WHY STREET STYLE IS A GREAT FEATURE

- It's inspiring to see beautiful images of individual girls and women celebrating their own unique style.
- It gives a handy insight into city-style from across the globe. You can witness what's hot in L.A. to everything that's going down in Tel Aviv at the click of a mouse.
- It frequently reminds you that there are no rules in fashion'I love to celebrate the rule-breakers!
- It's a great way to find specialized boutiques, designers or flea markets to pick up some fabulous unique pieces (see **Chapter 8: Pernia's Little Black Book of Stores**).

'Fashion changes, but style endures'

—Coco Chanel

1

WHAT IS STYLE?

Solène Debiès

One of the reasons why I love working in fashion, and why I wanted to write this book is because everybody has style. Everybody has an inner personality that they want to project to others. This isn't vanity or superficiality; it's a fact of life.

Rightly or wrongly, people make judgements and decisions about you within the first two seconds of setting eyes upon you. This, of course, doesn't mean you have to look objectively perfect every day (in fact, there's no such thing) but you should ensure that you are representing yourself faithfully and comfortably through the kinds of outfits you put together.

The best dressers I know have a fine understanding of their inner personalities which they translate into their wardrobe choices. They're able to reflect the best bits of what's inside them to the outside world. Sounds simple, haina?

I'm not talking about soul-searching here, but more a frankness with yourself about the kind of image you'd like to project.

Me?

I'm a girly-girl who opts for classic silhouettes in almost all of my wardrobe choices. I like to look feminine, but sophisticated. That's why you'll often see me in classic skirt shapes and shift dresses. I know what works well for my body and for the way I like to present myself to the people I meet.

Basic instinct...fatal attraction

Now I'd like to extend my mantra to: 'Know thyself, trust your instincts'.

One key way of deciphering your personal style identity is to go with what attracts you materially. Whether it's the colour, print or texture...stick with what you love. If you find yourself attracted to that bright pink floral dress, but you're hesitating because it doesn't neatly conform to the chicly monochrome vision you had for yourself you should still go for it! That impulse of attraction is a vital moment in determining your personal style.

We've all been in this position. Your friend (or worse, your date!) is waiting downstairs for you. They're ten minutes early and you're running ten minutes behind. Your bedroom floor looks like a well-rummaged stall at Sarojini Nagar market and your wardrobe is foaming at the mouth with a series of frivolous party dresses that you're snatching at but can't decide upon...

HERE IS WHERE YOU NEED TO TAKE A BREATH AND TRUST YOUR INSTINCTS, GO BACK TO THAT OUTFIT YOU FIRST ENVISAGED YOURSELF IN. TRY NOT TO OVER-THINK YOUR LOOK. WHATEVER YOU REACHED FOR INITIALLY IS PRETTY MUCH ALWAYS THE BEST CHOICE FOR YOU.

It's just as important not to mute aspects of your identity in dressing up as it is to overplay them. You can have as many 'you looks' as you want and unleash them onto the world. Can you imagine what a boring place that would be if everyone always dressed the same and according to trends? Speaking personally, I stay quite closely within the classic zone of dressing because that's where I feel comfortable, but once in a while I'll experiment with a cooler print or something on the grungier side if I feel like it.

It's not totally me but I'll do it sometimes because it's fun.

Sonam Kapoor is a perfect example of someone who can mix different looks to combine all of the crazy and brilliant elements of her personality. She's the most eclectic dresser I've ever come across. One day I'll meet her and she'll be completely punk and looking totally cool, sporting a studded jacket and big black biker boots. Then the next day we'll go for lunch and she'll have tonged hair, flicked out eyeliner, a poofy dress—so girly it'd make your heart melt!

Sonam is such a moody dresser; she really experiments

and it depends on what mood she's in. She's the perfect example of how one person can have so many different styles. You cannot pinpoint one thing and say this is Sonam's style and I love that about her.

So to be stylish you have to look inside yourself, recognize the multi-faceted parts of your character, and let your clothing choices reflect these. Trust your instincts but allow yourself to be flexible; with an extra inch of confidence you can try new things.

Strip down, take a look

But before that, I'm afraid you've got to get down to the basics.

Stripping down to your underwear and staring at yourself hard in the mirror may sound like an exercise in bizarre narcissism or perhaps military torture. However, self-knowledge regarding your body type is one of the fundamental pillars of being stylish.

You may love a mini skirt oriented, 60s style, but if your legs are your worst feature then you'll need to re-evaluate and channel the look in a different way.

It's so easy to look at pictures of stylish celebrities and assume that they all have perfect figures, remarkable self-control when it comes to eating and the most gruelling personal trainers on the planet (see: military torture). While the last one might be true, what these girls actually have is an encyclopaedic knowledge of_how to dress for their body. They know the stand-out strengths and wobbling-weaknesses of their shape (yes, even Kalki) and dress to emphasize or disguise these.

The natural curves of the human body contain more style than any fashion store. Remember that your body is the animating factor in all of your wardrobe choices, so it's important that you're frank with yourself and your size. Your clothing and body should never appear to be battling or straining against one another but mutually complementary.

I have so many friends who hide their beautiful frames in sack-style dresses because they think they're fat! It drives me crazy! Similarly, I know fuller-shaped girls wedge themselves into clothes which are two sizes too small.

IT MAY SOUND GLARINGLY SIMPLE BUT YOU MUST BE ABLE TO BE COMFORTABLE IN YOUR CLOTHES AND MOVE FREELY!

A stylish lady rarely shuffles and popped buttons can be a serious health hazard to those around you. (I do understand the occasional need for **discreetly** unbuttoning trousers after a large meal, but this should not be a daily occurrence)

My next chapter will help you to recognize which body type resembles yours most closely, and the different clothing choices which help you make the most of your personal shape.

British artist Wiliam Hogarth created a theory of aesthetics which celebrated the natural S-shape within the female form. S-Shaped curved lines signify liveliness and activity and excite the attention of the viewer as contrasted with straight lines, parallel lines, or right-angled intersecting lines which signify stasis, death, or inanimate objects).

Experimentation demands preparation

So you've had a good think about your inner personality, and a long hard look in the mirror. After reading my next chapter, you'll soon be an expert on what styles suit your body and what silhouettes are best to avoid. I'd say you are now safely in the zone of understanding your personal style.

However, what makes a person stand-out stylish is not always playing the safe card. If you can successfully experiment with your styles, whilst remaining true to your personal aesthetic, you will wow those around you with your flexibility, confidence, and sense of fun.

Still, I urge you to tread carefully in those wacky new shoes. See below for some guidelines on pushing the limits of your personal style without overstepping the boundaries.

❖ Sort yourself a soothsayer

If I really want to wear something new and I'm not sure about it, I always show my sister. She's the most brutally honest and blunt person who has ever lived.

You don't want someone who says 'you look good in anything' (husbands and boyfriends are, on the whole, not to be trusted) but someone who can let you know quickly and directly that there are four butt cheeks visible in those pants, or that somehow, yes, those shoes do give you the swollen ankles of an airhostess!

WHEN YOU ASK THE HONEST OPINION FROM FAMILY OR A CLOSE FRIEND THEY'RE NOT AFRAID TO OFFEND YOU. YOU CAN BE SURE THEY'RE BEING GENUINE AND WHAT'S MORE, THEY KNOW AND LOVE THE REAL YOU. IF THE SHOWCASING OF YOUR LATEST EARLY EVENING CREATION DOESN'T REFLECT THAT, THEY'LL LET YOU KNOW.

❖ Harness technology

Who could have predicted that WhatsApp would be one of the most effective weapons in a stylish girl's arsenal?

Few of us are actually fortunate enough to live with our guru who will point out exactly what is right or wrong with a new look.

For everyone else, there's photo messaging!

DON'T BE AFRAID TO PICK UP YOUR SMART PHONE AND SNAP A NEW OUTFIT THAT YOU NEED A SECOND OPINION ABOUT.

I do this all the time and have narrowly avoided some seriously disastrous purchasing decisions as a result.

An SMS equivalent of a thumbs up is all you need to carry your new look with aplomb.

Don't float an idea on a bloated stomach

As a dancer, there are times when I'm training like crazy in anticipation of a big performance. It's such hard work but it fortunately puts my body in amazing shape. During these times I tend to experiment much more in my outfits. With a healthy body I find that I'm more confident in my dressing and more willing to try new styles.

Recently, at the opening of Dirty Martini in Delhi I wore a backless fitted jumpsuit with a cropped top. On a bad day this look could have careered catastrophically into the Sandy from *Grease* disaster zone, but on that night it worked because I wore it my way and I felt good about myself.

Nobody loves their body all of the time, but it's important to embrace the moments when you're feeling toned and tanned to try something quirky.

> **WHEN YOU'RE FEELING CONFIDENT IN YOUR BODY YOU WILL EXUDE THE KIND OF CHARM WHICH CHALLENGES YOUR FELLOW DRESSERS AND HELPS YOU FORGET ANY EYEBROWS WHICH MIGHT BE RAISED AT YOUR FLAMBOYANCE.**

Fit your fashion to your feelings

As with your body, you should team experimentation with the right kind of temperament. Being nervous or unsure of your identity is not the time to experiment, and don't force yourself into experimental styles during this. Using erratic clothing choices to mask personal breakdown is so not stylish! See: Britney Spears' melt down circa 2008.

That's the time to meditate on yourself and your inner issues, not your wardrobe.

Despite this, you should recognize that when you're feeling low, honing your style and taking some risks can bring more comfort than any tub of ice-cream because you're doing something positive for yourself.

I had been going through a time recently where I wasn't been feeling the best emotionally but this really is the best moment to pick yourself up and get creative.

TRYING A DIFFERENT LOOK CAN PROVIDE A MOMENT'S ESCAPISM INTO AN UNEXAMINED, OR MAYBE UNFULFILLED PART OF YOUR PERSONALITY.

It feels good to discover different parts of yourself and dream up outfits accordingly.

If you pull it off (and with my help, you cannot fail) you'll find yourself boosted by the compliments showered upon you by your admiring and quietly envious friends.

❖ Take time to stand and stare

It's important that you allow yourself a decent portion of time to think your outfit through.

MEDITATE CAREFULLY ON WHERE YOU ARE HEADED (SEE CHAPTER 4: WHAT TO WEAR WHEN) AND THE KIND OF EXTERNAL HURDLES WHICH MIGHT ARISE FROM YOUR FORTHCOMING ACTIVITY.

For example, a picnic lunch date with your girlfriends is totally not the time to try out dominatrix stiletto heels. You risk getting stuck in the grass permanently. Shoe-icide! Instead use this opportunity to try a preppier look with white plimsolls or ballet flats.

Never forget that you are always at the mercy of the weather gods who are capricious, unforgiving, and will not hesitate to chastize you for an ill-planned outfit. Check the forecast an hour before you leave the house and assemble your look accordingly. The weather has the capacity to make you appear refined and elegant, or else a total fool.

Don't be stubborn—if you dress in ignorance of weather patterns, the probability of monsoon downfall or biting cold your outfit will look forced and inappropriate (see more in **Chapter 5: Seasonal Style**).

Accessorize with attitude

'What other people think of you is none of your business.'

Last summer I was in Paris for couture week. I was going to the Chanel show and I decided at the last minute to tie my sari with the pleats the other way round than it's conventionally tied. I pinned it up and skipped off to the show, unknowing of the media furore it would cause after my office tweeted a picture of me.

Suddenly I found myself on the front page of *Mail Today*! I was criticized for the experimentation; some fashion editors reprimanded me for misrepresenting India abroad. They felt that it was an insult to the sari tradition, they claimed that what I had dared to wear was akin to switching the colours of the Indian flag.

At first I was a little peeved. Who compares clothing to a national flag? But that's just the nature of dressing up. Not everyone is prepared to agree with your style choices, and if you take risks then people may talk and stare. The key to being stylish is learning how to rise above the whisperers in the corners. Whatever you want to wear you have to accessorize it with sassy attitude.

Living in Delhi, I've had to become immune to people staring at my outfits. When I moved back here from the States I found it so annoying and rude! Now I've come to a point where I can just block it out, because I'm not going to let anybody else make me feel uncomfortable. If people have a problem it's their issue.

Likewise, if you see someone working a kick-ass outfit, feel free to approach them and compliment them (I'm always asking people where they bought individual things) but don't stare. Allow those around you to express their individuality in whichever way they choose to—don't make them feel self-conscious! A truly stylish woman also presumes that those around her are stylish and would never be surprised to encounter another of her species.

Not all stylish ladies have to be non-conformists, but those who are manage to channel their inner Carrie Bradshaw, forget the critics and walk with an attitude of self-possession (even if inside you're deeply regretting the purple leotard and floor length kaftan).

❖ Hone your heroines

Don't be intimidated, get inspired!

We all have them. Let's admit it. Me perhaps more than anyone I know. You see them once and your heart starts beating uncontrollably, you want more than anything to be part of their world, to live a day in their shoes, to rifle through their personal belongings uninterrupted...

I'm talking about style crushes, of which I've probably experienced three times as many as the heterosexual kind. I think it began when I was at boarding school, rifling through *Seventeen* magazine (my bible) to get a glimpse at what my favourite actresses and musicians were wearing. Now I get my fixes on fashion blogs and even spying at parties, but I've also learnt how to exercise caution when I assemble my personal style icons, and I urge you to do the same.

There are certain celebrities who I admire so much and feel like we're on the same page style-wise. Kate Bosworth is a great heroine of mine. She is so simple and chic, to me her look is beautifully classic and feminine. When I was styling for my first movie, *Aisha*, I looked at images of many celebrities such as Diane Kruger and Kate Bosworth and based a number of my looks around them. To me they just look effortless.

Remember that style is not simply innate genius. We live in time where celebrities are in our faces every day and, used wisely, this can be incredibly helpful in determining your personal style.

AS MERE MORTALS, WE HAVE THE LUXURY OF LEAVING THE HOUSE WITHOUT OUR OUTFITS APPEARING ONLINE MINUTES LATER. CELEBRITIES, ON THE OTHER HAND, DO NOT. WORK THIS TO YOUR ADVANTAGE AND LET THE GLITTERATI EXPERIMENT WITH LOOKS FIRST.

Unsure if you should really team those yellow shoes with red Capri pants? Or whether riding boots off-catwalk actually look a little bizarre? Check online to see which of your fashion heroines might have rocked the look, or whether it's perhaps better confined to your dressing room.

Just as I've suggested you keep your copies of fashion magazines at arm's length, the most stylish way to channel your sartorial heroines is not to translate their look automatically onto your body. Kate Bosworth is a stick insect, while I have curves, so I tweak some of the outfits she assembles to make them work best for my body.

❖ Harbour your style heritage

'A thing of beauty is a joy forever'—**John Keats**

'If you were to gather all the clothes you have ever owned in all your life, each baby shoe and winter coat and wedding dress, you would have your autobiography'

—**Linda Grant**

Forget about celebrities for a moment and instead collect your inspiration closer to home. Every Indian girl has a stylish woman in her ancestry. Bright, exotic colours, rich textures and all-round flamboyance in female dressing has been a central feature of our aesthetic history for centuries, while most of the West were still pasting on lead make-up and dying their clothes brown!

There's nothing better than having somebody in your own family who inspires and influences you, whether it's an aunt, a long lost cousin or your great-great grandmother. I think it's so important to browse old photograph albums to draw inspiration from the romance and fashions of the past.

My heritage style inspiration is my grandmother. She hailed from a royal family, so she had a strict insistence upon beautiful clothing, accompanying this with her aristocratic attitude to style.

She inspires me because she cared so much for the rich quality of things, many of her pieces were made from real

My many birthday dresses and early fashion *adventures*

My grandparents in Pakistan; Nani is wearing a real silver duppata

Mom in her wedding dress

Mom's lovely vintage look

Mom at my college graduation

Mom in QOS

Mom goes retro

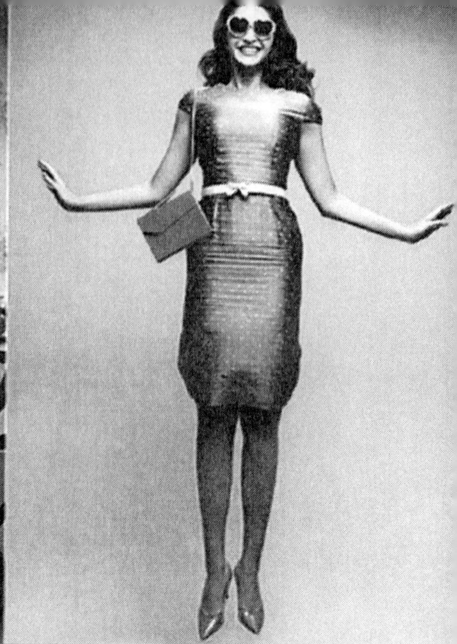

silver or gold thread. Can you imagine that sort of detail today? She was also happy taking charge of the needle and thread herself—it amazes me when I think of how she made my Mom's wedding dress by hand.

We still have so many of her clothes, they're works of art, family heirlooms to be cherished forever.

A BIG PART OF STYLE IS RECOGNIZING AND EMBRACING WHERE YOU CAME FROM. LOOK BACK AT THE WAY YOUR ANCESTORS PROJECTED THEIR OWN PERSONAL STYLE AND THINK ABOUT WHAT YOU CAN TAKE FROM THAT TODAY.

Take inspiration from your favourite fashionable family member and your style will be far more unique than an outfit crafted from celebrity magazines.

Some clever man in a US university once said that precursors were barriers to originality. While he was definitely talking about books and not the merits and pitfalls of luxe-bohemian dressing, he's got a point.

THE WHOLE THING ABOUT PERSONAL STYLE IS TO MAKE IT YOUR OWN.

We're all learning about style, just as we're always learning more about ourselves as we grow older each day.

Get influenced by celebrity style but not intimidated, gather inspiration from glamorous family members and decide how to make it new.

Great style is sincerity. Being stylish comes from knowing your heart, trusting your instincts, and expressing your personality with authenticity. It's about being frank about your body and dressing to its advantages. It's borne from maintaining a healthy distance from celebrity icons and fashion magazines and rediscovering your personal style heritage.

One of my favourite things about dressing up, is that no one has the right to tell you what to do. Before you proceed with the chapters that follow, you'll need to slap on layers of this attitude.

Whenever you leave the house, or sign your name on the credit card bill, look closely at yourself in the mirror. Analyse the contents of your dash around Forever 21. Ask yourself the question—is this me?

Once you're certain of that fact, I'm proud to announce that you are safely on your way to becoming stylish.

2

BODY SMART

'The dress must follow the body of a woman, not the body following the shape of the dress'

—**Hubert de Givenchy**

Triangles and squares, apples or pears—we all come in different shapes and sizes—but dressing beautifully for your body type can be a hard task to master. We are constantly bombarded with images of models and actresses clad in the latest trends and it's easy to pull a wincing face as we imagine these styles on our own frames. 'How on earth am I to pull off leather trousers when I'm 5 feet 2 inches?' Or 'imagine my bulky shoulders in this strapless dress'; we shudder inside and reach towards a comfortable pair of sagging leggings and boring t-shirt where we can brood in private.

Now, the purpose of this chapter is not to encourage you to leap into the next catwalk trend which rouses your amorous stirrings in your chest, but to show you exactly how you can make fashion fit your physique—whatever your frame.

THE MOST IMPORTANT PART OF DRESSING STYLISHLY IS BEING BODY APPROPRIATE; UNDERSTANDING YOUR BODY SHAPE AND PLAYING TO ITS ASSETS RATHER THAN EMPHASIZING THE FAULTS.

All too often we dwell on the negative in life, and this is especially true when it comes to our own bodies. Every woman suffers from low self-esteem and confidence at some point in her life, but it's vital not to let this negativity be directed towards your body.

Get fit

I get it, you're busy. You have an impending deadline, a meal to prepare, a plane to catch, a screaming child, but these are on no grounds long-term excuses for neglecting the health and fitness levels of your body. (I'm allowed to say this because I also try to use them from time to time!) The truth is that everybody needs to prioritize the health of their bodies as much as possible, regardless of external responsibilities. If you have time for Facebook, then you have time for exercise.

Your body is a temple, and you can proudly animate a shrine to the highest goddess if you treat it correctly. My philosophy in life is: 'if you don't like it, fix it'! Get proactive in your eating and fitness habits and you'll soon feel the glorious benefits inside and out.

THE FITTER YOU ARE, THE BETTER YOU MOVE IN CLOTHES AND THE MORE STYLISH SILHOUETTE YOU'LL CUT.

A stylish physique isn't about being tall, short, big chested or small—it's about being toned in the most visible areas, namely your arms and legs. Big bottoms, mummy tummies—these are easy to disguise. If you work on improving the tone of your limbs, you'll soon find yourself looking fabulous in an array of styles which were perhaps off limits to you before. The beauty of toning these areas is that you don't need an exclusive gym membership or the stamina of an Olympian to get active. Invest in a couple of 5 kg weights and use them regularly to get beautiful arms, which will complement anything you wear on your top half.

Likewise, legs. It's a truth universally acknowledged that mini skirts cannot look fabulous on everyone. But that doesn't mean you should hide your legs away; there is a skirt length for every body type and leg shape, so long as they're toned.

Evergreen secrets

Every stylish woman knows that there are a number of key items which, in conjunction with a good exercise routine and cherry-picked wardrobe choices, will make their bodies look fabulous. Lean in, girls, these are some of my most closely guarded secrets...

Secret #1: Underwear

> *'...a good bra can be one of the greatest aids a woman will ever know'*—**Caitlin Moran**

You know when you look back to pictures of women in the 1920s and further back? You're amazed at their dainty waist lines and fabulous cleavages and wonder how it happened that modern life made us all so comparatively bloated? Think again, my dears, because these women were reliant on some of the most constricting corsets and blouses imaginable. Their 22-inch waists came at a weighty cost which, more often than not, was 'breathing' and 'moving'.

Thankfully, these days we can forget the girdle in favour of some brilliant underwear which creates a hitherto unachievable sleek physique. Head to La Senza, Marks and Spencers or look online to find ultra-strong shapewear which will hoist and smooth your wobbly parts in all the right places.

SHAPEWEAR IS PARTICULARLY HANDY FOR FORMAL EVENTS WHICH REQUIRE TIGHTLY FITTED COCKTAIL DRESSES OR SKIRTS. THE PANELLED ELASTIC SMOOTHES YOU ACROSS THE MIDDLE, EVENING OUT YOUR CONTOURS AND KEEPING EVERYTHING TUCKED IN.

They tend to make you walk and sit up straighter and almost all designs have invisible seams to keep your knicker choice unseen to all but the well-trained eye.

I am a true fan of shapewear, and as a stylist I have borne witness to its transformative capacities on womens' bodies. But still, avoid using spanx to shoehorn yourself into a dress which would otherwise be far too tight—remember the scientific law of displacement and understand that they cannot work major miracles—just little ones. Oh, and, I would list spanx as one of those articles of female clothing that men are truly afraid of, so if it's date night, it's a wise idea to leave them at home...

Secret #2: Avail yourself an arsenal of feel-good cosmetics

I am a huge proponent of spoiling your body in as many luxurious creams and ointments as you have the time to apply. Who cares if that miracle cellulite busting oil doesn't really deliver the results you crave? The placebo effect gleaned from its application is basically equal to the miraculous cure it boasts to offer. Exfoliate and moisturize any piece of flesh you're planning to expose; if you prime your skin in this way, your limbs will appear more toned, glowing, and all-round delectable.

ANOTHER INGENIOUS TRICK IS TO USE BODY SHIMMER TO CONTOUR YOUR BODY TO LOOK MORE ANGULAR AND SLIMMER.

Sounds complicated?

Not so! If I'm going out somewhere I often use body make-up to emphasize the natural muscles and curves in my body.

Arms: hold one arm out and flex your muscles. Use a gel bronzer and paint in the sideline between your bicep and triceps using a foundation brush to blend. Repeat on the other arm.

Chest: using the foundation brush and gel bronzer, paint into the shadows around your clavicle bone. Next use a shimmery highlighter to accentuate your collar bones.

Legs: put on high heels, as this will naturally flex your calf muscles, and paint the shadows created under your muscles again with the gel bronzer and foundation brush to accentuate them. Next, take your shimmer and apply in a line down the centre of your shin bone—the slimmest bone of your leg will then protrude and capture all the attention.

Secret #3: Slimming shoes

> *'The fact is, sometimes it's really hard to walk in a single woman's shoes. That's why we need really special ones now and then to make the walk a little more fun'*
>
> —**Carrie Bradshaw**

No, I'm not talking about those gross trainers with weird weights that purport to lose you 5 kg in one week (so not stylish! For the record, trainers should be strictly Nike air max). I'm talking about the ultimate slipper than slims your legs, narrows your ankles and makes you walk like a supermodel.

The nude heel.

EVERY STYLISH WOMAN UNDERSTANDS THE SPLENDID SUPERPOWERS OF A NUDE SLIP-ON.

Its remarkable capacity to lengthen the leg stems from its chameleon qualities of blending into the skin of your foot and calf. Look hard to find the shade which suits the skin on your bare leg most accurately, and avoid ankle straps to lengthen the limb forevermore.

Secret #4: Confidence

Unlike hyper-elastic underwear and body shimmer, this isn't a closely guarded stylista-secret. We all know that the only way to be stylish is to present your outfit with as much confidence, sass and charisma as you can muster. But the real secret with body-confidence is to know that everybody suffers from a lack of it. Everyone has assets and everyone has flaws. Yet it still comes as a surprise to me when some of my most stylish clients happily reel off reams of negative attributes about themselves, which are practically invisible to anyone but themselves, and the voices in their head.

I believe wholeheartedly in the almighty power of clothes, but there are some problems, internal issues, which they cannot solve. Of course, a new dress, or great pair of heels can lift you when you're down, but you should not try and solve deep-rooted esteem problems with outfits.

What follows beneath are a set of guidelines (not rules!) to help you make the most of your body shape.

YOU CANNOT HEAD OUT OF THE HOUSE HATING YOURSELF. IN FACT, THAT'S MY ONLY GILDED COMMAND. IT'S ONLY WHEN YOU LOVE YOURSELF THAT YOU CAN BE TRULY STYLISH.

So how to attain a sense of high esteem about your body?

I know that this isn't a state of mind that you can just slip into like your favourite jeans. It will ebb and flow at different times, according to many other areas of your personal life, such as your career or family. The first, and most important thing in this is to have someone you can talk to about your problems and your esteem issues. It can sometimes feel vain to complain to someone about how we look, but we are usually doing this because of some darker problem inside.

Be good to yourself. Be better to yourself than anyone else. Exercise in a way that you enjoy; eat sensibly according to your body's demands, and not what you're telling it to crave. Try not to carry the burden of feeling a certain way.

INSTEAD SPEAK OPENLY ABOUT YOURSELF, AND SHARE YOUR FEARS AND FLAWS WITH FRIENDS—IT'S THE ONLY WAY WE CAN STAMP OUT OUR SELF-CRITICISM AND GET AN ACCURATE PICTURE OF HOW WE REALLY APPEAR.

Remember that even supermodels feel like they have hideous days. And those celebrities we see in magazines? Often they have just as many lumps and bumps as us! Yet how do they manage to transfigure into red carpet swans? The answer is simple, and the secret lies below. They know how to dress for their body type.

Body types

Apple frame: not as poisonous as you think!

As you progress through life it only becomes more difficult to obtain or maintain the kind of six-pack washboard stomach that we're bombarded with in magazines and movies. For anyone who has ever smelt a jalebi, or considered, however momentarily, children, then this is an unachievable ideal.

A lot of Indian girls are apple. The downsides are your rounded middle and big bust, but the upsides far outweigh these: slim hips, small bottoms, and lithe limbs.

IT'S A BODY SHAPE THAT I LOVE TO DRESS BECAUSE IT'S SO EASY TO BANISH THE BAD BITS AND GLORIFY THE GOOD.

My suggestions below are essential reading for apple figures because they skim over your doughy centre, saving you several hundred abs crunches per week and giving you the appearance of a skinny core rathar than spherical fruit. Hooray!

- **Tops**: Avoid, at all costs, plain top layers which cling to your middle. I include in this: tight vest tops, short t-shirts (which inevitably ride up), and stripes. Frills can also be fiendish by widening your bust—so keep away.

Instead opt for tops with ruching, a wraparound cut, and made from reasonably structured material which will stay in place. Floaty tops also look heavenly on you; providing they're cut just beneath your bust (empire line) and don't inadvertently cling to the wrong places. Don't be afraid to flaunt the cleavage which accompanies your larger bust; the flesh you'll flash in a v-neck will work wonders in balancing out your curvy bits.

- **Dresses**: Apple figures are made for dresses, and you'll have a wealth of styles at your sassy disposal. Opt for wrap dresses which drape distractedly over your thicker middle and tie at the side, drawing attention to your waist. I think every woman needs at least one Diane Von Furstenberg wrap dress; they're feminine, ultra-flattering, and effortlessly fuse evening and office wardrobes.

  As well as the wrap dress, an apple figure can do little wrong in a plain shift dress worn to mid-thigh; it will forget your frumpy middle and celebrate the slim arms and legs. Once you're clad in a great fitting shift, all that's left to do is accessorize!

- **Skirts**: One of the reasons why the wrap dress is so perfect for apple shapes is because of its voluminous skirt which flows out of the empire line. So I would advise that you also look for similar 'A-line' shapes for your separate lower half. I'm afraid that pencil skirts or anything body-con will cause problems as they'll maliciously cling to the stomach area. So think big and wear skirts on your waist rather than hips. It can also help to accentuate your waist area (therefore dividing your middle) with a belt; just don't wear it too tight or allow it to slim down onto your stomach.

CONTRARY TO POPULAR BELIEF, APPLES CAN WEAR MINI SKIRTS AND CAN LOOK HEAVENLY. JUST TEAM WITH A FLOATY TOP SO YOUR LEGS ARE THE CENTRE OF ATTENTION, RATHER THAN YOUR TUMMY.

- **Trousers**: Trousers can be tricky for apples to master, but there are some incredibly forgiving styles out there at the moment. Seek out flat-fronted styles which fasten at the side, and the higher the waistline the better

The cleverest apple frames understand that to pull off trousers with a-pommes (get it?) they have to disguise their midriff with a longer line top. Kurtas are your best friend in this occasion (when aren't they!).

- **Swimwear**: On the beach, a one piece is your closest ally if you have skinny skinny legs. If you have a broader torso then let the attention shift towards those beautiful lengthy pins! Avoid a sarong and opt for a shorter kurta so that your legs are still ultra-visible.

- **Jeans**: Ankle skimmers, skinny jeans. But the waist cannot be low or hipster. Make sure that your sides are snugly tucked in the jeans. Muffin tops peeking over your waistband is sartorial suicide and seriously uncomfortable.

Key item: Short shift dresses with sleeves in a soft material.

Pear: no nightmare!

Classically feminine, possibly the most ubiquitous female shape is the pear. How do you know if it's you? Well the chances are you've got narrow shoulders, a small bust, and slim waist. But below the hips it's a slightly different story—your thighs will be wider and, along with your bottom, this is probably where you'll find you put on weight most easily. In fact, it's pears who are most likely to ask:

'Does my bum look big in this?'

It might do...just a little...but if you follow my guidelines below, that dreaded question will soon be far from your mind.

- **Tops**: As with everything, it's important to focus on the beautiful parts of your body; the parts that you don't realize every woman in the room is secretly coveting. For most pear frames this will be your top half, which is usually beautifully slim. Pear-friends, I have one only edict for you: show this off! Ensure that the tops you buy emphasize your loveliest part and avoid hiding this in billowing, unfitted fabrics—smock tops may serve only to emphasize your widest feature: hips, so better to keep things ultra-fitted up top.

STRAPLESS TOPS, AS WELL AS SPAGHETTI OR EMBELLISHED STRAPS, WORK GLORIOUSLY ON PEAR FIGURES.

Your top half is the first thing that the eye sees, so make sure it's beautiful, and the eye will pass over the more shapely bits underneath. 'Bodies' are everywhere at the moment (no, not humans, but those tight tops which fasten between your legs) and while they can be fiddly on loo-breaks, they're a great option if you have a smaller torso. Plus, they fit snugly into those A-line, prom shaped skirts which I'll be recommending below.

Even if you're not a fan of your arms, keep them covered in tight fitting cardigans and jumpers which won't swamp you.

- **Dresses**: Strapless prom dresses are the most beautiful and classic dresses for pear-shapes. Skimming the waist and kicking out at your hips, no one knows if it's the cut of the dress or your hips which is giving such a beautiful shape. It's a classic example of dress and frame working beautifully to accentuate and yet disguise in the right places.

FLOAT LIKE A BUTTERFLY TOWARDS ONE SHOULDER AND OFF-SHOULDER STYLES, BUT SPEED AWAY FROM ANYTHING TIGHT ON THE HIPS; NAMELY MINI DRESSES. JUST BECAUSE BLAKE LIVELY WEARS IT, DOESN'T MEAN YOU SHOULD TOO.

- **Skirts**: As a pear, your weight will fall to your thighs, so your approach is as simple as this: steer clear from anything too short or tight. Instead, make sure your skirts have plenty of movement and don't cling to your larger lower limbs (pleats can help create movement). A-line skirts worn at the waist will accentuate this slim part of you. Ensure you don't wear any designs with pockets or embellishments, as these will draw attention to your widest parts.

- **Trousers**: Smart pears wear pants or jeans that kick out on the bottom. A flared leg draws the eye away from your hips and creates a more flattering line for your whole body. Keep your trouser-palate to the darker end of the spectrum and you cannot fail. Conversely, keep away from Capri or tapered pants which drive the eye right to the hips. I recommend pallazo pants and wide leg trousers.

- **Swimwear**: Girls with bigger hips call for thick-sided bikini bottoms made of a reasonably strong material. Keep a short, sheer sarong at hand for your cover-up—you can loosely knot it at your waist to keep your jelly at bay.

Key item: Pallazo pants or wide-legged trousers.

Hourglass: don't waist it!

It can be galling to hear hourglass girls complain about their figures, when their guitar-shaped bodies are typically thought to be the archetypal female frame. But many designers and high-street stores are increasingly cutting clothing patterns for a much more willowy, supermodel-style shape, meaning that hourglass girls cannot always bowl happily into any clothing style they fancy. Dressing this shape well relies on reinforcing the wonderful natural curves of your body, without getting too far into matriarch territory. It's about maintaining your balanced proportions and creating a womanly yet sleek silhouette.

- **Tops**: Make the most of your mid-section on your top half by tucking in t-shirts and blouses into high-waisted trousers or skirts. Avoid turtle-necks, which can give you a frumpy bosom. Beware that every curve of your torso will be reinforced, leaving little to the imagination with strapless tops.

- **Dresses**: So long as it's nipped in at the waist, almost any dress will glide over the hourglass body with enviable ease.

DRESSES WERE MADE FOR YOUR FRAME, BUT THEY MUST BE WELL STRUCTURED. WEAR FITTED CLOTHES BUT MAKE SURE THEY'RE NOT TOO TIGHT.

Consider going one size up so your clothes really mirror your figure, rather than pull at it. Steer clear of those 1920s drop-waist designs, and tread carefully with rectangular, shapeless shift dresses—both cuts risk emphasizing the hips disproportionately and unflatteringly.

- **Skirts**: The pencil skirt can look heavenly on your beautifully curvy body. Modernize this by tucking in a cute t-shirt or shirt, and keep your heels high to enhance the silhouette. Mini skirts are definitely an option, but keep an eye on hem lines and remember how easily they'll ride up onto your slimmer waist. Your body is so naturally sexy, it can sometimes be wise to play it safer in more classic designs.

- **Trousers**: A common mistake that hourglass frames make is letting their trousers or jeans fall too low on their hips, which emphasizes this contour disproportionally and can make you look dumpy. Keep trousers worn at your gloriously feminine waist with a good belt and make sure they stay there. Wide leg trousers will also delicately maintain the proportions of your hips and emphasize your fabulous, womanly behind.

- **Swimwear**: Hourglass babes can truly rock the one piece. I recommend finding a style which highlights your curves and even features cut away sections at the waist so that the whole beach can admire your contours. Opt for a cord kaftan as your beach cover-up—you'll need to belt the material slightly in order to keep your narrow waist in focus.

Key item: A belt to accentuate that wonderfully feminine waistline.

Inverted triangle

It may sound nowhere near as appealing as the hourglass, but the inverted triangle can be one of the most striking and powerfully feminine body shapes. This frame features wide shoulders, a small bust, slim hips and a subdued bottom, making it one of the most desirable body shapes, and that which you see most frequently on athletes and models.

The secret to dressing this shape well is by introducing discreet volume around your hips to balance your broader top half, statuesque rather than...

- **Tops**: I'm afraid that strapless boob-tube tops are going to be difficult to pull off, as will puffy sleeves and other shoulder detailing. This is simply because these features will emphasize your widest region. Instead, choose tops in floaty materials and avoid anything too stiff. Oversized V-necks in grey and black will look great on you, as will vintage inspired baggier vests which are cut low beneath the armpit. Button down shirts will also maximize your statuesque proportions in an enviably elegant way; just ensure you wear them open at the neck.

- **Dresses**: Tight sheath dresses with sleeves, mini dresses covered on top, and drop waist dresses will work like a charm.

- **Skirts**: The chances are you've got great legs, meaning you can wear shorter designs with gamine, effortless ease. Make sure you balance mini skirts with t-shirts or three-fourth length sleeves to keep your proportions in check. Don't shy away from midi or maxi skirts either! The dramatic ankle-skimming length will balance out your statuesque shoulders.

- **Trousers**: Skinny styles are perfect for your frame, and feel free to experiment with different colours and pastel shades.
- **Swimwear**: Seek out bikini styles with frilly or embellished bottoms. The extra material will give the illusion of slightly wider hips, in turn, narrowing your shoulders. On the top, triangle bikini tops suit your frame best. Mix and match your two-piece by choosing a darker shade on top and a brighter on the bottom to draw the eye downwards.

Key item: Drop waist dresses

Petite: all good things come in small packages!

Treading the line between petite-sweet and stumpy-dumpy can be a precarious business when you're 5 feet 4 inches and under. Designers are annoyingly fond of creating luxurious, draping garments that risk petites looking like they're playing dress-up. Petite girls must always be mindful of creating a lengthy silhouette; while those girls who are slight all over may also need to work on building curves through their clothes. Either way, my minute friends—walk tall! You're only as small as you feel and, as anyone who has received a Tiffany's box will know that the most stylish things always arrive in compact packages...

MAKE A BEELINE FOR ANYTHING WITH AN EMPIRE-LINE WAIST, BECAUSE IT TAKES THE NATURAL WAISTLINE JUST BELOW THE BUST WHICH GIVES THE ILLUSION OF HAVING VERY LONG LEGS.

- **Tops**: A plunging neckline will equally elongate the body by opening up your torso. Printed tops can look glorious on you but ensure the print isn't too loud or large—enormous flowers will only emphasize your contrasting stature.

- **Skirts**: Wear 'em high—a skirt with a high waistline will elongate the legs. Also don't be afraid of flashing flesh—petite girls are lucky in that they can get away with showing more skin than their taller friends without looking too trashy. It's a great way of getting noticed and preventing your clothes from swamping you.

REMEMBER THAT A SKIRT IN A DARKER COLOUR TEAMED WITH A LIGHTER OR BRIGHTER COLOUR ON TOP, WILL DRAW THE EYE UPWARDS, AND GIVE THE ILLUSION OF HEIGHT.

- **Dresses**: The two dresses which work best on you are the classic shift and the maxi dresses (as long as they are sleek and not too voluminous). The elegant draping of 1970s styles can work beautifully on your smaller frame and, providing you alter the hem, shouldn't drown you in swathes of fabric. If you're feeling bold then opt for something in one single colour—it will add inches to your height. Team shorter skirts with leg-extending pointy heels which finish low on your foot (just below the toe-cleavage line).

- **Trousers**: It's a myth that small girls shouldn't wear cropped jeans. Ankle-skimmers are by no means off limit, but they have to be just that—ankle skimming. Run a mile from any self-proclaiming 'Capri' pant, which finish higher up the leg and are perilous for any petite woman. High-waisted jeans which offer a slight flare are also a super option for shorter girls; tuck in your top to emphasize the waist and lengthen those proportions.

- **Swimwear**: Try same colour top and bottoms because different colours make for a stunted illusion. String bikinis will work.

Key item: High-waist silhouettes, for example, jeans, trousers, and skirts.

3

HOW TO SHOP

'Whoever said that money can't buy happiness simply didn't know where to go shopping'

—Bo Derek

My name is Pernia, and I am a shopaholic.

I've never been a smoker and I've never touched drugs; my singular vice is shopping (think what extra funds are available to me for not smoking!). I have a serious addiction, but fortunately I've been able to carve out a career for myself within the industry, which goes some way to masking the severity of the problem, although my close friends and family know the truth.

Well, to call it a problem or a vice isn't quite fair. There is a crucial difference between someone who is a spend-aholic and a shop-aholic. For a while, I was the former. As a college student, I would go shopping and gorge on the most frivolous things like a frenzied collector but I've now moved on from buying for buying's sake. Today, I will only purchase something if I really like it, if I've seriously considered the item and justified its place in my wardrobe. It just happens that I'm persuasive and I like a lot of things. This is what makes me a shop-a-olic.

CLOTHES SHOPPING IS MY PRINCIPLE PASSION BECAUSE IT'S ONE OF THE MOST EMPOWERING LEISURE PURSUITS A WOMAN CAN UNDERTAKE.

Like a carton of fine ice cream, it can be delightfully enjoyed alone but is perhaps better shared with friends.

We spend such a large portion of our lives making other people happy, whether it's your boss, children, or parents. But shopping is something that you do *just for you* and this inherent indulgence is one of my favourite parts about it. Asserting your financial independence and creatively expressing yourself through your purchasing decisions will boost confidence and incur endless joy, regardless of your budgeting constraints.

Shopping for the essentials

In the same way a chef's kitchen must first be well-stocked with the best spices and oils, so should your closet be properly kitted out with the basics. I'm not talking about dhania in your drawers, but a range of key ingredients that will make up the backbone of your wardrobe. These fundamentals are your primary priorities when you venture out to shop. If you get these basics right then you cannot *help* but be stylish in almost any given situation.

❖ Jeans: your second skin

Feminine but tough, practical yet sexy—every girl has to have one great pair of jeans, but this can be a chasm of confusion! It's vital that you get the right style for your body shape—they should flatter the worst part of your lower half and glorify the best (see **Chapter 2: Body Smart**).

SAVE LIGHTER, MORE AGED DENIM FOR A CASUAL LOOK, WHEREAS AN INDIGO WASH WILL FLATTER ALL BODY SHAPES AND TAKE YOU THROUGH DAY TO NIGHT.

Jeans shopping can be laborious but be patient, ask your friends where they like to buy their denim and research online if necessary. If you find a cut that works for you then do not hesitate to stock pile as many pairs as you can afford—finding that your favourite line has been discontinued can be extremely traumatic.

CR-326-BE

Fashion ideas for apple figures

Fashion ideas for **pear** *figures*

Fashion ideas for **hourglass** *figures*

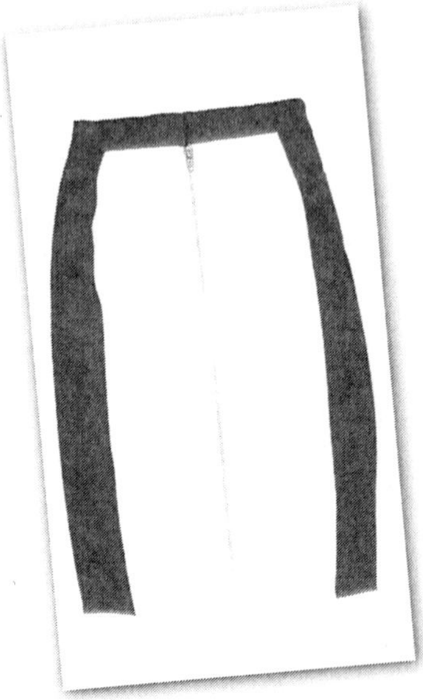

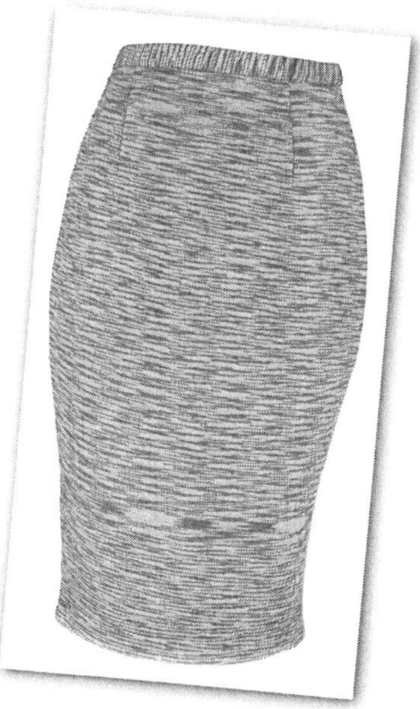

Fashion ideas for ***inverted triangle*** *figures*

Fashion ideas for **petite** *figures*

The 5 essentials that every girl must have: a LBD, nude heels, a camel coat, a floaty blouse and a white t-shirt.

WHERE TO BUY?

I love Levis and you can find them in almost any corner of the globe you find yourself. The sales staff are brilliantly helpful in helping you navigate through the different washes and designs. If you have a higher budget then J-Brand is almost unbeatable in fit and comfort. Zara do a great skinny jean in a range of colours, while in Topshop you'll find some great high-waisted cuts as well as boyfriend styles.

Think of a good white t-shirt as your fashion foundation

Just as with make-up, your white cotton t-shirt is an essential style-base upon which you can build prettier, more interesting things. Neglect this and your look could flake and crumble.

MAKE SURE YOU SHOP FOR SOMETHING THAT CAN BE USED IN LAYERING, BUT IS ALSO PRETTY AND WELL CUT ENOUGH TO WEAR ALONE.

(Just please let your subterranean layer be a nude bra) Look in Gap, H+M, Esprit, and American Apparel. So long as it's soft and well-fitted you don't need to spend a lot of money on this—you have food spillages to fear!

❖ In moments of distress, there's always the little black dress

Your little black dress is your partner in crime and your best friend. Stylish women turn to their favourite black dress time and time again because of its safety and versatility. Beware, however, of the term LBD—it doesn't always have to be a short length.

SHOPPING FOR THIS ITEM NEEDS TO HAPPEN MORE ORGANICALLY THAN, SAY, A JEANS EXPEDITION. LOOK OUT FOR STYLES WHICH SUIT YOU AND DON'T THINK TWICE ABOUT BUYING IT IN BLACK, HOWEVER SUNNY YOUR MOOD!

Black is naturally formal, slimming, and professional. What more could you ask of in a frock?

WHERE TO BUY?

Rohit Gandhi, Rahul Khanna, Pernia's Pop-Up Shop

❖ Flit stylishly in a floaty blouse

I recommend that you arm yourself with this highly feminine item as it can be endlessly flattering on your more bulgier days. Pastel or bright colours will suit your purpose best and can be teamed with jeans for a pretty, Marc Jacobs-inspired day-look. Whether it's button down, short or long sleeved depends on your personal choice but concentrate on the quality of the fabric.

SILK, ORGANZA, CHIFFON, GEORGETTE MAKE GREAT BLOUSES.

Even though they can be expensive, the returns are worth it as they will drape beautifully, helping you exude luxurious style.

WHERE TO BUY?

Snehla Khan, Mango, Zara, Gaurav Gupta, Pernia's Pop-Up Shop

Button up in camel

A camel-coloured blazer is a brilliant, versatile investment. Camel tones instantly instil sophistication and richness into your look, but will sit quietly behind your accessories if necessary.

Petite frames should avoid cropped cuts and pear girls should look out for a style with a structured shoulder to balance out their lower half.

WHERE TO BUY?

H+M, Banana Republic, Vero Moda, Nimish Shah, Pernia's Pop-Up Shop

Let your security blanket be cashmere...

A luxurious scarf or shawl is an absolute must. If possible, invest in cashmere. You won't regret the rupees when you're cradled in its softness. This will be like the security blanket you carried around in your infancy! Take it travelling, throw it over your LBD, or cuddle up at home in colours which will brighten up your denim or camel basics.

I WOULD SUGGEST A BASIC COLOUR BUT PINK IS ALWAYS CHEERY, AND A LEOPARD PRINT WILL LOOK CONTEMPORARY BUT STYLISH.

WHERE TO BUY?

Janavi, Ezma, Pernia's Pop-Up Shop

❖ Regional representation

Every Indian girl needs one beautiful, classic sari. Think traditional rather than trendy here, and a design which showcases the famous textiles of your region. Not only will you be upholding your local craft but your outfit will tell a story—wearing a chikankari sari if you're from Lucknow shows respect and reverence for your culture. And as we saw in Chapter 1, there's nothing more stylish than embracing heritage.

WHERE TO BUY?

Abu Jaani Sandeep Khosla, Ekaya, Pernia's Pop-Up Shop

❖ Sole basics

A pair of nude and black heeled pumps will compliment any number of outfit combinations. Nude colours are such leg lengtheners and mean you always have a pair of shoes to match your outfit. Keep the black pair by your desk so that you can quickly smarten a work outfit should you need to.

YOU CAN USUALLY CHOOSE BETWEEN MATTE AND GLOSSY FINISHES BUT I RECOMMEND MATTE AS THE GLOSS CAN SCUFF AFTER POUNDING THE PAVEMENTS.

Metallic sandals are also a vital part of any Indian girl's wardrobe. If you have slim ankles then go for something that highlights this lovely asset, perhaps a gladiator style. If your legs are on the chunkier side then go for an open style so your calf is not cut off from your foot.

WHERE TO BUY?

Charles and Keith, Aldo, Louboutin

For pumps, try Steve Madden and Aldo (their sales are excellent) as well as British brand Kurt Geiger, which has recently launched here. Your local market will stock many styles of sandals but specifically DNA and Venus Steps at South Ex market in Delhi always has an impressive range.

Almost all of these items can be mixed and matched to come up with something extraordinary. Your beautiful shawl, teamed with a smart camel jacket, and your LBD could work for you in so many different contexts. Keep these basics beautiful, ensure you're never without one of them and you cannot fail to be well prepared and stylish at any occasion.

If you find your wardrobe is lacking in any of these, then I'm afraid it's time to hit the shops.

How to shop

> **Carrie**: *'Honey, if it hurts so much, why are we going shopping?'*
> **Samantha**: *'I have a broken toe, not a broken spirit.'*

There's never a day when I don't love shopping. In fact, if this day ever comes I know that things are serious, really serious (quick and simple cure: fly me to New York!).

However, recent studies show that over half of you can find shopping highly stressful and so I've drawn up a few tips to help you treat the experience more positively, and see it less as a chore.

Tip #1: Prepare yourself

The first mistake people make is shopping only when they need something urgently. This is not to say you should spend money on things you don't need, but if you see something you love, pick it up. There is nothing more vexing than shopping to find a perfect outfit on the day of an important event. You end up running around like a headless chicken trying to prise yourself into a pair of pants which look dreadful and that you secretly detest. This sucks all the joy out of what should be a pain-free and pampering experience.

DON'T MAKE THE MISTAKE OF ALWAYS BUYING GARMENTS *FOR* AN OCCASION. INSTEAD, THE OCCASION SHOULD FIT YOUR *EXISTING* COLLECTION OF YOUR FAVOURITE CLOTHES. I COLLECT STYLISH THINGS THAT I LOVE SO THAT THEY'RE READY WHEN THE MOMENT COMES.

Tip #2: Select your spree-day and outfit wisely

Think carefully about the time of day when you're venturing out to shop. It's better to wait a fortnight or longer between expeditions, than to navigate your crowded local market on a Sunday afternoon. If you can, use a quiet weekday evening to browse the mall. There is nothing more off-putting than spending half of your allotted 'spree-time' in the queue for the changing room.

SIMILARLY, DO NOT GO SHOPPING IN JEANS OR BOOTS. WEAR SOMETHING LIKE A DRESS AND FLATS WHICH YOU CAN SLIP ON AND OFF WITH EASE.

It's also good to avoid wearing obtrusive underwear at all costs—trying on a beautiful frock only to be distracted by the prominent frills of your panty-line is just a shame, and a waste of your (and the dress') time.

Tip #3: Pick a shopping partner

Personally, I'm quite happy to shop alone, but if you're indecisive then you should take someone with you who you trust. Don't let yourself be accompanied by someone too sensible because the activity should be fun (mothers often fall under this category).

SOMEONE WHO CONTINUALLY REMINDS YOU THAT THE FUR GILET, OR WHICHEVER SLIGHTLY FRIVOLOUS ITEM YOU HAPPEN TO BE CLUTCHING, JUST ISN'T WHAT YOU *NEED*, IS BEST LEFT AT HOME, OR FOR VERY SEVERE WORK WEAR SHOPPING BINGES ONLY.

Also, remember that in their eagerness to make a sale, asking the opinion of a store attendant will rarely bring an honest answer to your style query.

Tip #4: Be smart in a store

Don't let merchandisers make a mug of you!

I strongly advise you to trust your instincts when it comes to where you shop. Only you can know which stores suit your body and personal price range the best. What I do urge, however, is that you mix and match and try not to buy everything from one store. (If your time is limited to one shop then make it a multi-brand store, such as Pernia's Pop-Up Shop where you can easily browse and shop from different collection.)

Like I said with fashion magazines, it's good to look at stores' campaigns to get inspiration, but don't download the window display of your favourite store onto your body. The chances are that the window dresser is nowhere near as stylish as you can be!

Shops will always arrange their clothing on hangers or displays to show you how all the pieces they're selling can work together. This is the job of the store merchandiser whose sole responsibility is to cross-merchandise together in order to coerce you, the consumer, to part with your well-earned dosh. So if you catch yourself admiring one skirt at a distance, then snatching up item after item thinking you're making some miraculous, Nobel-worthy style-discoveries, hold onto your shopping basket for a second and exhale quietly. This capsule outfit you're collating, comprising pieces conveniently positioned parallel to each other could be about to render you style victim.

Looking like a walking talking manifestation of H+M or Esprit's spring collection is not going to win you any style followers. You will look one dimensional. It's so obvious and disappointing when you see a glamorous looking woman from afar, but when you get up close you realize she's simply adorned herself in clothes gleaned solely from the front display of Zara.

SOMETHING ABOUT BEING STYLISH DEPENDS ON SECRECY. MIX AND MATCH YOUR LOOKS FROM DIFFERENT PLACES—INTRODUCE THE ODD UNEXPECTED ITEM SUCH AS A FAMILY HEIRLOOM OR SOMETHING THAT YOU PICKED UP ON YOUR TRAVELS.

This will add texture to your outfit, you'll ooze originality and, most importantly, you'll look like you.

Tip #5: Observe, enjoy

A stylish and smart shopper observes and browses before she buys. I love to browse in expensive shops, study their mannequins and window displays, and then see how I could recreate certain looks from high street stores. This is becoming much easier to do nowadays as the high street has become increasingly assiduous in copying high-end collections. Mango and Zara are two stores who are almost faultless in their interpretations of designer pieces.

EVEN IF YOU DON'T HAVE STACKS OF MONEY BURNING A HOLE IN YOUR JEANS, THERE'S NOTHING WRONG WITH GOING OUT AND BROWSING. IF YOU FIND SOMETHING YOU REALLY LOVE THEN KEEP IT IN YOUR MIND.

I've got a fatalistic approach to shopping; I feel like if it's meant to be in your possession then it will still be there when you finally decide. (For everything else, there's eBay—it can be really helpful to browse eBay to ease your pain when you've missed out on a gorgeous sundress that you were quietly admiring. Be prepared to pay up to 20 percent of the original price, as the vendor will often charge according to the scarcity and beauty of the item.)

As well as delighting in the delicious panorama of clothing rails which stretch before you like an unchartered kingdom, take a look at your fellow shoppers and soak up inspiration from their style too. The eclectic clientele of certain stores, such as Topshop London (otherwise known as high street Mecca), can help to stimulate your style senses. If you're unsure of whether a certain look could work, take a look around you and see who is experimenting too!

The cognizant consumer: even Bergdorf babes have to budget!

There are times when you will dash into a shop, select something on impulse, and it will become part of (your wardrobe's) history. But buying on impulse, as euphoric as it can feel, should be a naughty exception rather than the rule.

Here is where I get serious. For all of the creative expression, the experimentation, and primeval urges that contribute to your purchase decision and despite the necessity to spoil yourself, there is an ultimatum you have to face when you leave the dressing room, a little giddy, five items in hand. This decision has a binary and absolute outcome: *can I afford this?*

If buying one jacket will result in you making mad adaptations to your lifestyle such as: 'It's okay if I buy this outfit, I can just survive the rest of the month eating plain rice—I'll look skinnier that way!' or 'it's fine, who pays their "rent" anyway', then you need to stop, put down your credit card, and get yourself a glass of water (leaving the shop is also effective). It's so easy to be swept up in that swirling twister of consumerism only to be spat out after the storm with an array of expensive clothes but no means to show them off.

MANY GIRLS FIND SHOPPING STRESSFUL BECAUSE OF THE GUILT FACTOR. THEY FIND THEMSELVES IN DIFFICULT SITUATIONS WHERE THEY END UP BUYING SOMETHING THAT THEY CAN'T AFFORD. BUT TRULY STYLISH WOMEN KEEP BOTH TIDY APPEARANCES AND TIDY ACCOUNTS. THEY BUDGET.

When I was student and also when I lived in New York for my first job, I had to be highly attentive to my finances to ensure my shopaholic tendencies didn't get me evicted. Each month I would draw up a spreadsheet which divided my incomings into necessary outgoings. Anything apart from food, rent, or phone bill that was remaining went into my shopping pot. It wasn't much, but I was clear about how much I could spend. Within these limitations I could shop in peace.

You don't have to spend it each month, if you have any left you can buy something more expensive the next time (this has never happened in my personal experience!).

'Never give up on something you really want. However impossible things seem, there's always a way'

—**Sophie Kinsella**

There are very few people who can purchase everything that they want immediately. Even very wealthy women have to shop within some financial constraints and so you have to be realistic when you're pining after those shoes that just seem as if they were *made* for you. Saving up for an item that you've admired for a while can be one of the most empowering and eventually satisfying processes of shopping. The time you take to save your rupees will ensure you've carefully evaluated the seismic effect that particular garment will have on your life, and you can be confident that you'll get lots of wear out of it.

A COMMON MYTH THAT I'D LIKE TO DISPEL HERE IS THAT ONLY ITEMS PRICED LIP-TREMBLINGLY HIGH CAN BE CONSIDERED 'INVESTMENT PIECES' (*FASHION SPEAK). THIS IS INCORRECT. IN FACT, ANY PIECE OF CLOTHING THAT YOU BUY IS AN INVESTMENT IN SOME SENSE.

Nothing is more wasteful than the top you picked up for Rs 1000 but which sits in your closet unused. If you take five minutes in the fitting room to envisage your wardrobe and the different clothes you could pair with it.

WEARABILITY IS KEY TO INVESTMENT, AND IT HAS MUCH LESS TO DO WITH THE ACTUAL PRICE OF THE GARMENT THAN YOU THINK.

The shrewd shopper

So you're approaching the counter with the amazing frock, you're confident that you've got the cash and that it will work with hundreds of shoes, handbags, and jackets which are lying dormant in your wardrobe. You've even got to the point where you're envisaging successful dates, triumphant job interviews and high-fives from all your friends, just for wearing the thing. In these last moments I want you to do just one last-minute quality assessment. Sounds technical, but what I mean is check the quality of the garment.

NEVER BUY ANYTHING THAT IS SUB-STANDARD. I LOVE HIGH STREET SHOPPING BUT EVEN THEN YOU HAVE TO CHECK WHETHER IT'S GOOD QUALITY OR IN GOOD SHAPE.

Make a mental checklist of the following, and if you have serious doubts over more than one area then think about spending your rupees elsewhere...

❖ Feel the fabric

If you're paying a sizable sum for an item, make sure that this is reflected in its fabric. You can go to your local textile shop to familiarize yourself with what feels expensive and what sells for a cheaper price. The more aware you are of the wholesale price of the fabric, the more clued in you'll be over your bargains. Make sure you're getting a fair deal. Avoid anything too shiny or obviously synthetic looking if possible.

❖ Be diligent over detailing

Check the garment's detailing, its buttons and seams. Ensure that nothing is missing. If the item is heavily embellished, check to see if the jewels or sequins fall off easily when you try it on. Equally, super-sequinned items often require stringent (and expensive) cleaning procedures. If you'll need to dry-clean something regularly but you know from your past history that this chore always somehow eludes you then think twice about buying it.

❖ Fit! Fit! Fit!

There is some excellent tailoring available on the high street, but you need to be a savvy shopper to track this down. If you're buying a jacket, *check how the shoulders and lapels are made*—do you think it will hold its shape after a few months? Flimsy clothes that don't hang well will never earn you style points.

Online shopping: how to?

Over two decades ago, a British genius/geek named Tim Berners-Lee invented something called the World Wide Web, designed for sharing information between computer systems. I wonder whether he could have ever predicted the impact that his technical perseverance would have on all of our lives, everyday and forever more.

In comparison with the search engines, the games, and cyber networking, web users were initially cautious about shopping for clothes online. When Natalie Massanet founded Net-a-Porter in 2000, potential investors scoffed at her conviction that yes, women would part with their cash over the net for beautiful things that they hadn't touched or tried on. How they underestimated the innate female capacity for imagination and expenditure!

I started Pernia's Pop-Up Shop (www.perniaspopupshop.com) in 2011 because at that moment there was no website which captured the unique experience of boutique shopping in India. Women were able to shop online from international sites but they couldn't access the incredible breadth of Indian designers who were out there. I wanted to showcase our home-grown talent, not just domestically but to the whole world! (We now regularly receive orders from the States, Europe, Middle East, Asia, Australia, and even as 'far out' as New Zealand!)

PERNIA'S POP-UP SHOP IS A GREAT PLACE TO FIND SEVERAL DESIGNER LABELS IN ONE PLACE, SAVES A LOT OF TIME.

There are new styles available everywhere or few days which is not a feature in physical shops.

While I will be eternally fond of 'foot-browsing', I am a convert to this church of e-commerce. It's brilliant to witness the increasing numbers of people across India taking the sartorial plunge and ordering online. Women no longer have to trek to larger cities in order to get their hands on beautiful pieces, and this convenience factor is particularly persuasive.

We all live very busy lives but with online shopping you can have this amazing pleasurable experience without having to take out a massive chunk of your day—it's so convenient!

'L'enfer, c'est les autres' (Hell is other people)—Jean-Paul Sartre

If you are a shy shopper and crowds nauseate you, online shopping means you can browse much more happily in private (by this I mean in pyjamas). That irritating pressure from pushy sales assistants gets deflated, you can stare at a dress for three days and no one's going to tell you to hurry up!

What's more, you can also scan your wardrobe to see what will go with the items you're browsing and to check whether you have something similar already.

For those uninitiated, web shopping can be intimidating, but follow these guidelines and you'll soon find little nuggets of style appearing at your doorstep.

AND, OF COURSE, WE ALL KNOW THAT THERE'S NOTHING MORE EXCITING THAT GETTING A PRESENT, EVEN IF IT'S FROM YOURSELF.

Self control

The first point might sound obvious, but I need to safeguard myself against the financial ruin of you all. Whatever you buy online WILL APPEAR in physical form (great!) but you will unfortunately be charged for it! It's easy to overspend because you're purchasing privately and no one is raising an eyebrow at your excessive basket contents.

DO YOURSELF A FAVOUR, DISABLE THE OPTION OF ONE-CLICK SHOPPING.

Engage all the cognitive powers we discussed earlier. Do not shop online when you are sleep-deprived or drunk. If you're feeling a tad weepy however, online shopping will quickly help you find your smile again.

Only shop from trusted sites

Global banks have made huge strides in protecting your card security online. Usually your bank will request a password before the site can weasel funds from your account. That said, exercise caution about where you shop. Unless they are trusted brands, foreign boutiques may not have to adhere to the same security measures that you're familiar with and could be risky.

❖ Enlist the zoom!

Only shop from those sites which have detailed photography of the garments. At Pernia's Pop-Up Shop we feature a powerful zoom in order to bring you into as close contact with the garment as possible. You can use this to study the fabric of the product closely and cross reference this with the information that the retailer provides in the product description.

❖ Measure up

Ensure that you know your exact measurements so that you can be sure the garment will fit you. If you have further questions about the product then go ahead and call customer service to get the exact dimensions. The online shop isn't a faceless machine and you have the right to ask anything you want. Truly excellent e-tailers, such as Pernia's Pop-Up Shop, will offer in-house alterations to ensure you get the perfect fit!

❖ Abandon your fears

If the item you ordered didn't match up to your wild fantasy then worry not—you can simply return the item in the post and receive your refund promptly, without question. If you order with Cash on Delivery and can change quickly enough—you can send it straight back!

My favourite online haunts

www.perniaspopupshop.com
www.netaporter.com
www.shopbop.com
www.asos.com

4

WHAT TO WEAR WHEN

Solène Debiès

Dressing for an important event is a delicate balancing act, a wobbling tightrope between standing out spectacularly and deftly blending in with the general ambience of the occasion.

These are the outfits for the make-or-break moments in life that you remember forever—the first date with your future husband, your best friend's wedding, or that job interview you aced. So whatever you do, don't leave your clothing choices to the last minute. Looking appropriate is about much more than stylish intuition; it also requires elements of careful thought and planning.

Date dressing

Looking stylish on a first date is a task of towering proportions. You can try to persuade yourself that your date will focus on your riveting tales of rafting in Rishikesh or incisive views on Kashmir but a date is one of the few occasions where you can be certain your outer shell will be studied and scrutinized by even the most blinkeringly doting of dating partners.

So what's a girl to wear?

A successful date outfit will fuse elements of delicate femininity, quiet self-confidence, subtle sexuality, and infinite charm. It's about creating the perfect platform for your magnetic personality to perform upon.

As with all occasion dressing, make sure ahead of the date that you're familiar with the locale of your engagement.

DON'T BE AFRAID TO ASK HIM ABOUT WHERE YOU'RE GOING, AND CHECK WHETHER YOU'LL BE INSIDE OR OUTSIDE SO YOU CAN DRESS ACCORDINGLY.

Research the venue: has he suggested somewhere chi-chi for cocktails or a dive bar for beers? Check the place out online and finely tune how casual or smart you should be.

Of course, what you should wear is dependent on what you feel comfortable in and where you're going, but do keep a few things in mind when you're collating your date outfit.

❖ Firstly, don't downplay your femininity

I hardly know any men who don't love a feminine girl and this is because this is what they're most familiar with.

They will have grown up surrounded by women who have adhered to a strictly gendered dress code and while you may love experimenting with androgyny, a first date is not always the best occasion.

REMEMBER THAT FEMININE DOESN'T NECESSARILY EQUATE TO 'GIRLY' DRESSING. TURNING UP IN HEAD-TO-TOE PINK, BOWS, OR OVERLY-CUTESIE THINGS WILL MAKE YOU LOOK LIKE A PRECIOUS BIMBO.

Instead, opt for classically feminine silhouettes such as a wrap dress or a-line skirt which enhances your waist. If you're wearing trousers, soften this look with a floaty blouse to contrast with your tailored below.

Emphasize your femininity in clothes that highlight your beautiful form but don't reveal too much of it

Deciding on the degree of flesh you should unleash on your date can be an enormously tricky business and it's something you should consider carefully before stepping out. Show too much flesh and you'll look like you're trying too hard. What's more, you'll be attracting the guy for the wrong kinds of reasons—not a good idea if you're looking for more than just a hook up.

Try to introduce a balance of the amount of skin you show

The ancient lore is if you're showing your legs then keep your top half covered, and vice versa. Make sure that the flesh you do reveal is the best for your body shape and think creatively about other zones of your body that might be appealing. Make a feature of your back, for example, with a top which is cut lower on that side. In the same way, a delicate necklace worn with a simple vest or t-shirt will draw admiring glances to your collar bones and neck rather than your cleavage—much more stylishly alluring than a push up bra and low cut top.

Other parts of the body that are underrated:

- Wrists
- Back
- Neck
- Shoulders

Titillate but don't intimidate

It is with a heavy heart that I must warn you to avoid anything too uber-stylish or trendy on a first date. As sad as it sounds, generally speaking, men can be intimidated by unique and directional dressing and most will not appreciate your outfit's nod to Balenciaga Spring Summer 2013 in the same way your female friends might. Relationship experts warn that directional clothing choices can be short-hand for 'high maintenance'—and may cause your man to run in the opposite direction.

IN A RECENT POLL ABOUT WOMEN'S CLOTHING, JUMPSUITS, LEGGINGS, HAREM PANTS, AND TUXEDO JACKETS CAME TOP IN ITEMS OF WOMEN'S CLOTHING MEN HATE. NOT FORGETTING, OF COURSE, UGG BOOTS.

Don't scrub these out of your wardrobe picture forever, but stick to classical styles which will be familiar to your partner.

Mane-tenance

A key indicator of fertility is hair, and 82 percent of men think it's a crucial part of a woman's sex appeal. This is cause for celebration during date dilemmas as you can comfort yourself in the knowledge that your clothes will matter much less than you think. In fact, if you're getting ready in a rush then it's actually better to focus less on your dresses and more on your tresses.

Avoid a hairstyle which looks too severe; although you want him to gaze cooingly into your eyes, a high scraped bun or poker straight hair can look a little intimidating and rigid.

TRY TO WEAR YOUR HAIR OPEN AND INTRODUCE A LOOSE WAVE EITHER BY PLAITING IT WHEN IT'S WET OR SETTING A FEW ROLLERS AS YOU'RE GETTING READY.

Also remember that boys love braids. If you want to keep your hair out of your face then tie some braids and fix them to the sides of your head for a soft and feminine look.

Whatever your hairstyle, make sure it looks glossy and healthy. How else do you think Kate Middleton bagged her British prince?

AVOID

- **Any clothing with a slogan**: Your 'bitch from hell' t-shirt may be amusing to wear in bed but you don't want him to discover this fact too early on.
- **Your push up bra**: It will distract him for the wrong reasons.

- **Boyfriend jeans**: First you need to bag the boyfriend.
- **Flat shoes**: Unless it's a daytime date then wear heels, even if it's just a small wedge. You'll walk with more sass and ooze confidence. (Save your super high dominatrix heels for a later date.)
- **Coloured tights**: Men are afraid of them.
- **'Statement' lipstick**: Keep make-up neutral and natural. You need to look like you! Steer clear of purple or red lipsticks for the meantime, they present a plethora of anxiety—inducing, smudgey risks.
- **Texting at the table**: For tonight, your phone belongs in your bag. No live updates to your friends and certainly no tweeting.

'I believe that happy girls are the prettiest girls'

—**Audrey Hepburn**

Remember that the most stylish girls accessorize with attitude. Smile, be breezy, don't fiddle with your hands and, if you're in a bar, stick to two glasses of wine. The second date will swing around in no time.

Meeting the parents

You know that *Friends* episode where Phoebe goes to meet her new boyfriend's parents? She wears an Alice band, a twinset with pearls, and asks in a faux American accent, '*So where does everyone summer?*' Phoebe usually has a kooky, bohemian style but decides to dress like a preppy American Republican to impress Mike's parents with hilariously disastrous consequences.

Meeting the family is a tricky business, in India perhaps more so than any other country. In our society especially, it's essential to keep good relationships with your boyfriend's parents if you want your own relationship to flourish.

FIRST IMPRESSIONS HERE ARE IMPORTANT. YOU HAVE TO STRIKE THE RIGHT NOTE BETWEEN SELF ASSURED YET APPROACHABLE.

The mistake that Phoebe, and so many others, make is dressing to impress the parents; trying too hard to be something they're not. Of course, you need to look smart and respectful, but also like you! While you may think that his parents will be impressed by a traditionally dressed Indian girl, don't feel under pressure to dress this way if it isn't how you usually roll.

What I do advise is to dress one notch more conservatively than you would on your first date. So if you wore a beautiful blouse and jeans then throw on a cardigan. If the blouse was quite sheer, make sure you wear a vest underneath.

LOOK TIDY AND SMART BUT NOT TOO FORMAL, YOU DON'T WANT HIS MOTHER TO FEEL UNDERDRESSED!

Key giveaways are your nails (keep them manicured) and your handbag.

YOUR HANDBAG IS A TRUTH ABOUT YOUR CHARACTER UNIVERSALLY ACKNOWLEDGED AND COMPREHENDED BY ALL WOMEN. TURNING UP WITH A BATTERED TOTE BAG WILL INDICATE TO HIS MOTHER A CERTAIN SHABBINESS IN OTHER AREAS OF YOUR LIFE. YOU DON'T HAVE TO BE HEAD-TO-TOE IMMACULATE, BUT DO KEEP YOUR ACCESSORIES MATURE, SLEEK AND POLISHED.

One tip is to wear something, such as an item of jewellery, which holds some sentimental value or has a story behind it. Then it can be a conversation piece at dinner (all the better if it's a family heirloom!). Add tidy hands, natural make-up, and clean hair to the clothing equations below and you'll soon be the daughter they never had!

Jobs

'It is an interesting question how far men would retain their relative rank if they were divested of their clothes'

—**Henry David Thoreau**

Lately, dressing for work has gotten a lot more complicated. With many companies now operating a smart casual dress code, gone are the days when you could don a trouser suit and be office ready.

What's more, gender politics in the workplace is a prominent issue for all females and affects the way you should present yourself at the office.

Although I'm sometimes envious of the ease with which men can just throw on a suit as a universally acceptable uniform, stylish girls understand and celebrate the fact that women no longer have to dress as men in order to get ahead at work.

In the past, your level of professional ambition was measured in shoulder pads and dowdy hemlines, but these days 'power dressing' is much more subtle. (As a side note: women are often 'accused' of power dressing. This is because they are intimidated. If this ever happens to you do not treat it as an accusation but simply smile and thank them for the compliment. All stylish girls dress for power in some way.)

MY FIRST TIP TO MAKE SURE YOU ARE WORK APPROPRIATE IS TO IDENTIFY ONE WOMAN IN YOUR OFFICE THAT YOU THINK IS SUCCESSFUL AND CHANNEL HER WORKPLACE STYLE.

I don't mean that you should go out and clone your boss' wardrobe, but pay attention to what the smart working girls are wearing and keep your outfits along the same lines. Follow her rules and limitations around footwear, the tights/bare legs conundrum as well as hemlines and you should avoid any serious fashion faux pas.

Corporate

Career chicks in the corporate sphere have to dress conservatively. It's a mournful but unshakeable fact. Many of my lawyer girlfriends had to battle hard in their early careers to be taken seriously in a corporate environment, so they opted to dress as maturely and demurely as possible. The aim is to bowl over your colleagues in the boardroom with your professionalism and sharp intellect, rather than distracting them by your directional and flamboyant wardrobe.

WHETHER IT'S A JOB INTERVIEW OR YOUR DAILY WORKING LIFE, YOU WILL NEED TO BE SEEN TO FIT IN WITH THE BRAND OF THE CORPORATE ORGANIZATION, SO YOU HAVE TO SAVE YOUR WARDROBE EXPERIMENTS FOR THE WEEKENDS ON EVENINGS.

The palate that you should keep in mind when you're shopping for work should be formed of whites, blacks, navy blues, and greys. Neutral wardrobe is recommended with accents of colour if needed.

Instead of light, polyester grey opt for a gunmetal tone, which looks much more contemporary and feminine. And unless you want to look like a banker from the last global recession, I would avoid pinstripes—they can look dated, cheap and seem to go hand-in-hand with dandruff.

White shirts are your wardrobe staples—try Banana Republic, Gap, or Mango for some great fits and make sure they are always tucked in.

WATCH OUT THAT THE MATERIAL ISN'T TOO THIN SO THAT YOUR UNDERWEAR IS VISIBLE, BUT EQUALLY AVOID ANYTHING TOO BULKY THAT WRINKLES UNDER YOUR SUIT JACKET—IT'S

WORTH SHOPPING AROUND TO GET THE MOST TAILORED FIT TO YOUR BODY.

Trouser suits are your safest and most conservative suit option. A great way to modernize this silhouette is to find a suit with slightly cropped trousers; just make sure the shoes you're revealing are polished (I recommend Oxford pumps) and the heels are no higher than three inches.

If you want to add in a splash of colour to your outfits then tread carefully; this is certainly not the domain for your make-up—instead keep colour to accessories. I think a coloured scarf can add interest and depth to a corporate wardrobe, but make sure it's not too flashy. Luxurious stationery is another great way of demonstrating your stylish personality and boundless taste in a subtle way. See smythson.com

Lastly, don't let your employer be distracted by your beautiful, flowing hair; keep it tied up and out of the way. A brushed ponytail can look just as elegant as a bun, but ensure your hair is tidy and out of your face and your dazzling corporate prowess will radiate through.

❖ Smart casual

A smart casual office can actually be one of the hardest dress codes to roll with. Again, watch your colleagues carefully to see where they tread, but you can let more of your personal style into the equation. The knack is to stand out but also blend in...

In this kind of office, you can usually get away with jeans, so long as they're smart. I recommend going for a darker denim wash and a well structured fit because this looks smarter.

Footwear can be a bit of a minefield, so I suggest erring on the side of smartness. Some offices will be fine with trainers, but as a general rule I would avoid wearing them with jeans as they can look sloppy. If you wear flats or sandals make sure they are structured and smart, flip-flops are a big no-no.

THE SMART PART OF SMART CASUAL DEPENDS ON YOUR GROOMING AND GENERAL CLEANLINESS, SO MAKE SURE SHOES ARE POLISHED AND YOU LOOK TIDY.

What I recommend is to take the basics of a working wardrobe and twist them slightly. So wear a pencil skirt with heels, but swap in a smart white t-shirt for your button down white shirt, and accessorize with a colourful scarf. Similarly, take your tailored trousers and white shirt but add a colourful or printed blazer to demonstrate your individuality.

❖ Fashion

I'm lucky enough to work in a fashion office, which is very different because you can wear pretty much whatever you want. When I went to my first fashion interview for *Harper's Bazaar* in New York, I remember wearing an oversized Miu Miu sweater with opaque tights and crazy wedges. When they're applying for a job in fashion, many girls can get intimidated by the dress code. They feel that if they want to show they're dedicated to fashion then they should turn up clad in designer gear from head to foot. This is a myth I'd like to bust right here!

The fashion industry is very accepting, and when I interview girls I can rarely tell whether their sweater is market-place or boutique bought. If you're interviewing for a role as stylist or buyer then your outfit should reflect your individuality since you may need to be prepared to talk about where you sourced your items from.

If you're applying for a role in a shop, make sure your look is aligned with the kinds of clothes you'll be representing. If it's a fun, youthful store then wear colour and if possible, something from the collection itself.

My last piece of advice?

Look *ambitious*. Dress for your next job, not the one you're in. You'll soon be sashaying stylishly up that career ladder.

Girls' night out

Dressing up for a night with my girlfriends is my favourite kind of occasion dressing! It's so much fun because it's all about you. It's indulgent and silly and exciting. I always try to give myself a pampering session beforehand.

Run a bath, condition your hair, and have a glass of wine while exchanging outfit ideas with your friends over text.

AN OCCASION LIKE THIS IS WHERE YOU CAN LIVE OUT YOUR WILDEST FASHION FANTASIES.

There's more than a little bit of showing off involved, and your clothes can be a talking point between you all. Your friends are the crowd who really appreciate your personal style and can give you feedback so don't hesitate to experiment a little with a bold lip or crazy heel. Let your accessories be unadulterated and your outfits more risqué if you want to.

If you're going out to a bar or club in a gang then this where you can pageant your tighter and sexier clothes—my girls' night uniform last winter was an amazing pair of high-waisted black leather pants, which were so tight they only belonged after dark. There's safety in numbers and scores of men to dazzle so don't be shy to show a little flesh!

One rule: as cute as it looks in the bedroom before you leave, coordinating outfits are best left to boy bands and hen parties, so steer clear.

Student style

This is an important lecture, so listen up! When I was a student there were countless occasions when I trotted off to the library in college wearing sweatpants, pulling an all-nighter, and looking gross. I admit that. As a student you face so many essay crises and nighttime exam scenarios that these moments will be unavoidable—your hair will be greasy, you'll be clutching a bar of chocolate, and your eyes will carry the look of a frightened rabbit.

But, student readers, we all know that the library is the centre of campus life, and you inevitably meet all your college there, including the cute guy you've had your eye on all term. So wherever possible, let these sweatpanted, greasy days be an exception rather than the rule.

This is not to say that you should bypass comfort altogether, in fact this should be your primary concern when you're dressing for the library. During winter terms, oversized knits can be your go-to item as they're super chic, cosy, and comfortable. Pair them with nice tights or skinny jeans with some ballerina pumps or brogues. In the summer, opt for a loose shift dress which isn't fitted, and flats. You don't need to accessorize, you're there to work, not jangle!

Preppy outfits are the order of the day on campus, and while you don't want to look like you've looted your college gift shop, showing your affinity with your school can be so much fun. A university hoodie (look for a vintage wash) or college scarf shows you're proud to belong. The most stylish students can experiment with vintage denims, t-shirts, and day dresses for understated chic—but mix vintage with contemporary pieces to avoid overdoing it.

As a student, your budget is going to be limited—so you have to get experimental. Seek out the best local thrift stores, markets and find out which shops offer student discounts and when. Take some campus initiative and organize a college clothing swap amongst friends. Ask everyone to bring along ten items of clothing that they don't wear anymore and you'll soon have rails of second-hand treasures to browse through. It's a great way to get rid of your old stuff and pick up exciting new pieces for free!

Tip: Ask everyone to bring Rs 200 as donation to a local cause and you've organized a stylish and simple charity fundraiser.

Gym bunnies

In recent years we have seen a huge improvement in the styles of sports clothes available for women. Where previously designers balked at lyrca, sweatpants and sneakers, we now have fusion ranges such as Stella McCartney for Addidas which offer technologically advanced yet stylish gym wear.

Never underestimate the motivational power of a great gym outfit. If you feel stylish when you exercise, you'll work harder and achieve rewarding results.

Visiting the gym, I'm often struck by how many people work out in ugly and oversized clothes—I can't understand it!

AVOID THE TEMPTATION TO HIDE YOUR BODY IN LOOSE FITTING CLOTHES THAT SWAMP YOUR BODY'S OUTLINE.

Although being affronted with your lycra-clad form can be a little intimidating at first, it's important to know what your body looks like. Why? Because then you can actually watch your body change shape—it's so uplifting to watch yourself grow fitter and more toned.

As well as getting you better acquainted with your body, tight clothes help you move more easily. Say if you're doing a certain squat, your butt is supposed to go down a certain way and rise up another way. You need to see if you're doing it properly and fitted clothes help you monitor your movements and get your technique right.

A good sports bra is essential to help you maintain this sleek silhouette. A breathable vest top, which offers further in-built chest support teamed with breathable running leggings is your basic look. Stick to dark colours on the bottom and light on top so that, should you sweat (heaven forbid!) it will go unnoticed.

Stylish exercise bunnies understand that this is the time to go hair up and make-up free; don't clog your pores, let your skin breathe.

Nike, Adidas, and Reebok. This trinity of brands is famous for a reason (see Planetsports for all three) and I strongly recommend visiting the proper sports outlets for your gymwear—don't accept cheap imitations. The authentic material needs to be breathable and stretchable for your impressive movements and exertions.

Weddings

The Indian wedding is an unparalleled extravaganza of style and splendour. I love to take in the panorama of colours on display, the beautifully draped saris and exquisite jewellery. It leads me to one overwhelming conclusion: no other country does it better.

With wedding dressing we are lucky that there are traditionally tried and tested dressing formulas that we can turn to so we will always look appropriate. In my opinion, it's not in the dressing that issues arise in matrimonial style, it's the *under*dressing.

WEDDINGS ARE FORMAL AFFAIRS, AND DRESSING FORMALLY IS A WAY OF SHOWING YOUR RESPECT TO THE HOST. TURNING UP SCRUFFILY DRESSED OR (SHAME ON YOU!) IN JEANS SUGGESTS YOU'RE NOT TAKING THE EVENT SERIOUSLY— A STYLE ABOMINATION!

For the wedding itself, I advise you to choose traditional outfit combinations, since this is the most conservative event. Whether you opt for sari, lehenga, or shalwar kameez depends on your personal preference and, crucially, your comfort. Where you can have a little more fun is with the sangeet. I love the way Indian women have been experimenting with East and West fusion styles for this party—it's a great way to show your flair for dressing and individuality. Remember that you'll be dancing at the cocktail party, so tie your sari well and plan your footwear accordingly.

I recently wore a hot pink neon sari to my cousin's wedding with a really tiny blouse. I tied it a lot higher and wore it with flats so I could dance in it. Sometimes flats are necessary but if you can be certain you won't collapse inelegantly on the dance floor then try heels, which look best with saris and make you look sleeker and longer.

Fusion dressing allows you to blend the best bits of Eastern and Western fashion. Achieve the balance correctly and it can be a heavenly union.

Tip: Keep your tikka in place with eyelash glue!

5

SEASONAL STYLE

There is not much you can do against the fancies of nature.A clear blue sky can turn treacherous and metamohrphosize into a downpour before you've finished your cup of coffee. What you can do is to be prepared with some priceless fashion advice to weather-proof your style.

Monsoon

The season of frizzy hair, heavy-sky headaches, and clammy skin. But that doesn't mean your wardrobe should suffer as much as you do. You know that this season is going to swing around year after year, so there's no excuse for you to get caught out in a shower which drenches your sass and style in an instant. As with occasion dressing, you have to be prepared.

Your key shields against the onslaught of H20 are few in number and will work for you year after year.

The trench

The great thing about trenches is that they exude effortless style, and come the monsoon months they'll keep you warm and dry. A piece of twentieth century fashion history—the trench was developed as a light alternative to the heavy coats worn by British and French soldiers in the First World War. The invention of this unique design is ardently contested by designers Burberry and Aquascutum, but it is the designers at Burberry who have continually adapted and re-imagined it to keep it fresh.

If possible, invest in one for daytime and one for night. Simply chucking on the same rain-soaked and mud-splattered mac you wore all day to an evening function is just not stylish. Both trenches should be long enough to cover you, but unless you're aiming for a Matrix-style silhouette, I don't recommend full length.

A COAT WHICH FALLS JUST BELOW YOUR KNEE IS PERFECT FOR THE DAY, THOUGH AT NIGHT YOU COULD OPT FOR SOMETHING SLIGHTLY LONGER.

Typically, trench coats are double breasted, but if your décolletage is larger than others, avoid looking too boxy by opting for a design which unbuttons centrally. These coats should be worn looser rather than super tight, they still have a masculine connotation and that can be fun to experiment with. If you feel like the coat is swamping you then simply tie the belt at the waist to give you a neater shape.

Stick to a reasonably versatile colour for your day-trench.

Camel is the traditional shade but you can brighten up those thundery skies with a more vibrant colour; just make sure it's practical in terms of your footwear and handbag.

Many stores are now making beautiful evening-trench designs in some luxurious fabrics. While your day-trench must be durable, try a night time version with lace detailing, or a more structured frock-coat shape. Just avoid anything too embellished or fussy, the most attractive part of the trench is its timeless simplicity.

BEST WORN WITH:

your favourite jeans, sleeves scrunched up, and your collar turned out.

NEVER WORN WITH:

any other item of 'military' paraphernalia.

Rain boots

How many pairs of shoes have you ruined getting caught in the monsoon?
How many times have you sworn to yourself it will never happen again?

The worst thing about this season is that gross sensation of wet feet. So get damp-smart by investing in a sturdy, dependable pair of welly boots. The Queen of England's favourite brand is Hunter, and it happens to be mine too!

The trick with wellies is to ensure your chosen style leaves enough space between your calf and the boot. Bulging legs over the top of rubber boots is so not stylish! And, as tempting as it may be to indulge your inner mad old woman by scooping up a pair of natty coloured boots, I recommend sticking to the traditional colours of green, blue, and black. If you're desperate for a way of brightening up your monsoon outlook then opt for a single bright colour, but remember patterns can look slightly naff.

REMEMBER...

- Heels on welly boots are a classic example of a fashion faux pas borne from unsuitable embellishment. A heel on your rain boot suggests that you are open to the possibility of slipping in the mud or toppling in a puddle. In other words, ridiculous.
- It's vital to remember, amidst all this, that wellies are a stylish *solution* to a metrological inconvenience. They are not to be proudly worn in the office or at a cocktail party, so make sure you don't forget your spare pair of shoes!

Oh, and one more thing which is your secret weapon against these tropical storms. A bottle of hair serum should never be further than 3 feet away from you at all times during this season. Always wear your hair up and use this miraculous formula to slick down any protesting bits of frizz. You'll soon be ready to splash in style!

AVOID

- Plastic kagools (unless you want to look like a tourist).
- Anything white (unless you are a major exhibitionist).

Summer sun

I just love getting dressed on holiday. Firstly, you feel beautiful. You're well-rested, in good shape and—so long as you've been diligent with your SPF—your sun-kissed skin should be glowing like the moon on the ocean. It's the perfect time to take pleasure and time over your outfits. If you're on holiday with the girls then it's also the moment to get generous—share the contents of your suitcases with each other and experiment with different clothes and styles.

Summer holidays

Stylish girls on summer holidays are suitcase smart and recognize that they don't need to pack all their favourite clothes. In fact, it's likely that your most prized items from daily life will not be suitable for lying out in soaring temperatures. So leave those items behind and instead carefully select a few hot weather essentials.

AVOID THE TEMPTATION TO VENT YOUR HOLIDAY EXCITEMENT AND BLOW YOUR BUDGET ON A SHOPPING TRIP THE DAY BEFORE DEPARTURE.

If you invest in a few key summer items then you can be beach-ready at any point with an hour's notice. (Should the invitation come along...any offers?)

SUMMER HOLIDAY PACKING LIST

Take with you:

- **2 x swimsuits**: Choose a style which is best-suited for tanning. I usually take a bikini and a one-piece (see Chapter 2: Body Smart to find the best style for you).

- **Cover ups**: Your favourite white kurta is perfect for this. Then pack a coloured kaftan and one in a print. Opt for Aztec or digital prints over florals to gain maximum beach admirers. Team with luxurious sandals, and a big cocktail ring for a relaxed evening look.

- **Shorts, linen trousers, or palazzo pants**: A pair of cotton shorts in a light material will work for both the beach and the bar. Linen trousers or wide legged trousers (palazzos) are incredibly chic if you're less comfortable with baring your legs. Pair these with a plain coloured tank top and hoop earrings for a gorgeous 70s beach look.

- **Tank tops**: Pack these in plain colours and in abundance. Keep the style simple and embellish with jewellery instead.

- **Hat**: Floppy beach hats are so elegant but should remain on the beach. If you're heading out somewhere, then opt for a fedora style which better suits city day trips and jaunts into town.

- **Party dress**: You need to pack at least one party dress which won't crease and which works well with flat shoes. Now is the moment to go for something tighter and fun, in a colour which will show off your lovely skin.

- **Accessories**: Ethnic jewellery looks amazing on holiday, especially in colours such as turquoise, gold, and coral. Pack at least two pairs of statement earrings and necklaces to dress up your wardrobe. It's also always smart to scavenge for original pieces on your trips, as locally-crafted jewellery often looks the most appropriate. Take one small relaxed clutch bag, like a wicker clutch bag for when you're heading out.

- **Light fabric**: Take your cottons and chiffons with you. The lighter the fabric, the more comfortable you'll be.

- **A good book**: Lie supine with a stylish book that will get you noticed more than anything else. *Tender is the Night* by F. Scott Fitzgerald and *Bonjour Tristesse and A Certain Smile* by Françoise Sagan are classic beach reads.

Leave behind:

- Anything too fussy—ruffles, bows, etc., look too try-hard in the heat.

- Anything in leather.

- Anything that can only be worn with punishingly high heels—if it's a relaxed holiday you won't wear them.

- Anything too tight—your skin will be sensitive from the sun so be gentle to it.

In transit

How much fun is people watching at airports? Everyone does it—it's so interesting to check out what people are wearing and imagine where they're headed. So looking stylish at the airport as well as at 30,000 feet is a vital part of your summer style genesis.

But this doesn't mean you should dress for a cocktail party—heels are not compulsory! Look airport appropriate and dress comfortably but not scruffily (draw the line at sweat pants and Ugg boots). Donna Karan has the most amazing line of cashmere clothing for travel and I love to take a Hermès blanket on board, but it needn't even be so luxurious; jersey materials and snugly scarves will keep you warm in those freezing cabins. If possible, get hand luggage which complements your main suitcase—this, combined with your darkest shades, will give you an ultra-sleek aesthetic as you speed off into the skies.

Winter

This needn't be the season of fashion discontent as it is in other countries.

The Indian winter is, on average, a short-lived affair. It's your golden opportunity to showcase your wardrobe's thicker fabrics and its heavier embellishments that would otherwise make you swoon in the summer heat. My advice is to revel in the lovely, muted hues on offer in winter collections. Choose mulberry, chocolate brown, and teal tones over neon or clichéd Christmas red.

HOSIERY FOR BETWEEN-SEASON FINERY TIP

Invest in three pairs of good quality opaque tights for the between season months. Woolford tights are amazingly comfortable, but whichever brand you buy ensure they are suitably thick (60 denier and above) and adequately stretchable. Buy one above your usual size because they can shrink easily in the wash and, to be truly comfortable, they'll need to finish at your waist. Pair your tights with your favourite summer dresses and you'll weather the transitional weeks with easy-breezy style.

Boot(y) call

For many women, finding the perfect pair of boots is a lifelong quest which we undertake with saint-like fervour.

Why are we so obsessed?

Of course, boots are a fundamental pillar of style but they are also a psychological buffer against the onslaught of winter; we feel that we can weather the harshest of cold spells, provided we have a sophisticated layer of leather beneath our knees.

Along with your basic heeled pumps and ballerina flats, the winter season calls for two pairs of boots: your flat boots and what I affectionately term, your little bootie.

Flat boots...

...are a totally sleek and stylish winter footwear choice. These boots are delightfully comfortable, and therefore most definitely made for walking. Your flat boot ushers in a glorious dimension of versatility to your wardrobe, acting as a warm layer to wear with your favourite skirts and dresses in cold weather. Make sure that the leather isn't too tight around the leg (leave around half an inch of room) and that they finish at a flattering point on your calf.

SHORTER GIRLS SHOULD CHOOSE A LENGTH WHICH ENDS JUST BELOW THE KNEE CAP RATHER THAN MID-CALF.

For an injection of Parisian chic try the straight-legged riding boot; otherwise sturdy biker boot styles work well here, so long as they're kept polished and sleek.

Try your favourite flat boots with a mid-length dress and bare legs for spring and autumn. That little flash of flesh is a great way to harness the inherent sexiness of a great pair of boots, without having to overdo things in thigh-highs and hot pants.

BOOTY TIPS

- Many flat boots feature sheep-skin detailing on the exterior but beware of winter filth! That lovely cream is unlikely to last, so think twice before you invest.
- Experiment with your beloved flat boots and team them with a matching pair of knee-socks to elongate them.

Booties

These boots are made for partying!

Booties are typically worn at the ankle and feature a mid-length heel. When purchasing these charming shoes take care not to be seduced by anything too high as they'll need to accompany you day to night. Opt for a thicker heel over something with a stiletto and you'll increase their wearability threefold. Booties work for evening events such as drinks in a bar or a dinner party as well as a smart-casual dress code. If you're short of leg, ensure your boot finishes low on your ankle; a 'shootie' style is one level above a pump and can add inches to your legs. Hooray!

TO TUCK, OR NOT TO TUCK?

Tucking a great pair of jeans into your boots is a global phenomenon and can look highly stylish. But there are a couple of caveats to avoid looking like Puss-in-Boots. Firstly, your jeans have to be skinny enough to fit easily into the top of your shoes. This look also works best with a dark and flattering shade of denim such as indigo. Shorter and curvier girls should ensure that their boots have a heel—however slight—to avoid looking dumpy. Always balance this tight lower half with something floaty up top to level this silhouette.

Knitwear

Tread carefully when stepping into knitted territory and keep your body shape at the forefront of your mind. Be aware that wool can be a difficult fabric to wear and risks adding inches to your body size, so if you're larger or particularly short, avoid heavily knitted items.

But that doesn't mean all knitwear is off limits to you; in fact curvy girls will look gorgeous in well-fitted, lightweight woollens in darker shades that emphasize body shape and delicately skim over curves. If you're larger up top just make sure you wear something with a V-neck line to avoid the boob-shelf effect; steer clear of roll necks too!

Taller and willowy girls can get away with chunkier knitted pieces much more easily. You just have to take care to wear a more fitted item on your lower area such as skinny jeans or opaque tights to balance out your baggier half. Avoid looking like an ageing fisherman by choosing contemporary, bright colours—neons, canary yellow, and emerald greens work beautifully on Indian skin tones.

Cashmere is the warmest and most luxurious knitted fabric out there, but it can also be expensive, difficult to maintain and sometimes *too* toasty! Nowadays there are some beautifully soft and good quality alternatives in the market. Gap offers many pieces in Merino wool, which is both light weight and incredibly warm.

Remember that wool is a natural fabric whose timeless aesthetic can be cheapened by synthetic or artificial embellishments. Avoid glitter threading, an excess of fluff and, heaven forbid, anything with baubauls.

WOOLY TIPS

- A round necked, navy blue or baby pink cashmere sweater is an incredibly useful and chic item to pick up. If you wash it carefully (i.e. by hand and not more than 30 degrees centigrade) it will last you for years. Layer over a white shirt and team with pearls and jeans for a classic and feminine daytime look.
- A long, fitted grey cardigan is a key knitwear item, which will take you from lounging on the sofa to lunch with your girlfriends. Its softness makes it perfect for Sunday-style while the tight sleeves and dramatic length ooze laidback elegance. This neutral shade will work with countless items in your wardrobe.
- Knitted dresses are a brilliant one-step solution to your style SOS moments throughout the winter. Best teamed with tights and flat boots, knitted dresses provide instant winter chic and drastically minimize that foot-hoppingly freezing window between leaving your bed and getting dressed .

How to layer

Layering needn't be the fashion headache it's deemed to be. In fact, there are so many articles out there which over-complicate the matter, leading some to perceive it as a sacred dark art, understood by few and misinterpreted by many.

In reality, layering is as simple as putting your clothes on. It's just that in winter months this requires a little more coordination than usual.

The keys to layering are texture and colour. If your look comprises the same colour or material, you'll risk looking heavy and a little overdone. Instead introduce different materials into your layers by mixing cotton with jersey, or denim with lace. The cuteness lies in the contrast.

- You should always base your layered look over a lightweight, tight fitting top. Neutral colours or stripes work well, as do lace camisole vests.

- Next, add your thin cardigan or jumper. V-neck styles work well, as do hooded jumpers. Experiment with colour and texture at this point—try a bright neon or ribbed jersey.

- Lastly, apply your outer layer. This could be a blazer, leather jacket or long cardigan. Ensure it's a neutral colour and try to contrast it with the lengths of your previous layers. A cropped blazer over a longer t-shirt or jumper can look amazing.

...and not forgetting! Layering cries out for the liberal application of accessories, in most circumstances, a great scarf or shawl. Here is where you inject the last dosage of boldness into your outfit: find a printed scarf whose pattern echoes the colours of your layers—even if it's just one.

Apply this basic approach and, like your favourite sandwich, your layered look will artfully combine disparate elements to mouth-watering effect.

TIPS

- Apply layers only on your top-half. Lower layers may include thermal underwear but the less said about that the better.
- Umbilically attached to your favourite party dress? Make it work for daytime by teaming it with a tight fitting black t-shirt à la British style icon Alexa Chung.
- Oversized denim shirts are a useful relaxed layer to throw over a vest and jumper as denim will work with any number of different colour combinations!
- A coloured hoodie beneath a black leather biker jacket will keep you stylishly snug.

- Crisp button down white shirts, belted cardigans beneath a boyfriend-cut blazer can be a great layered look for the office.

Which coat to choose?

The winter coat is a much fussed-over topic, when in reality it's a simple art form. Beware of excessive fashion magazine reading, advising you on this season's 'must have' coat in blood orange or mustard yellow—these shades are so restricting that your poor garment will remain indoors for the majority of its daring existence. As boring as it may seem, your winter coats need to be in neutral shades to ensure their longevity in seasons to come.

❖ *The cape*

Once the sole domain of medieval bandits and Little Red Riding Hood, the cape has been much updated to give you a superhero spring in your step through the winter period. Like the trench, it has a distinctly cavalier, dramatic silhouette; its implied masculinity only serves to emphasize your femininity.

This is such a useful item because you can throw it over whatever you're wearing, wrap up and feel warm. Or, for the transition weeks, leave it open to feel cooler. Worn over a biker jacket or thick jumper, the cape is a versatile layer offering a hint of snugness rather than a full winter coat which can often be boxy, restricting, and too hot.

ENSURE YOU WEAR THE RIGHT LENGTH CAPE FOR YOUR HEIGHT.

Petite girls can get engulfed by the swathes of fabric so ensure it fits your shoulders and ends no lower than mid-thigh. Team with a LBD, opaque tights, and heeled booties for a sleek winter ensemble.

Pear figures should opt for a belted cape to balance out their lower half, while bigger breasted woman can opt for the more modern twist of a cape jacket.

Hoods on any winter clothing is totally practical and can be extremely chic (especially if fur-lined.) The cape is no exception; seek out a piece that can also keep your ears toasty and, more importantly, protect your blow-dry in the spell of crisp cold.

❖ *The evening coat*

The lovely slouchiness of your cape is not suitable for smart evening events, where you need a coat with a little more structure and warmth. Your coat shouldn't be so thick that it crushes your delicate evening outfit, but it does need to be a good deal warmer than your day cape.

There are many beautiful evening coats out there which are like outer dresses, with inbuilt skirts that flare out. While these look glorious on top of a dress with bare legs, if you're investing in one smart winter coat then you need something which works with both skirts and trousers. A straight cut is a much better option in these circumstances.

As with your cape, keep the shades of your coat neutral and avoid too much embellishment, save that for your party dress underneath. Instead, score subtle fashion points by seeking out winter coats with larger lapels, beautiful linings, or interesting cuff detailing.

INVEST IN THE HIGHEST QUALITY EVENING COAT YOU CAN AFFORD. BUTTONS ARE AN EASY INDICATOR OF QUALITY, SO ENSURE THESE DON'T LOOK TOO CHEAP (PLASTIC LOOKING, OVERLY SHINY, SLIGHTLY WOBBLY OR SMALL). IF THIS IS UNAVOIDABLE THEN BUY A BETTER LOOKING SET AND STITCH THEM YOURSELF.

Tall girls shouldn't be afraid of experimenting with the length of your coat. A sweeping outer layer that falls mid-calf can add a significant degree of drama and elegance to your evening look.

Petite girls, on the other hand, will need to look more carefully at their hemlines to avoid looking swamped.

Ensure the arm-length is correct and seek out belted styles to give your frame more shape.

Finally take care of your winter clothes, girls

Knitwear, heavy coats, and footwear all require some TLC at this time of year. Hang your coat up *properly*—don't sling it on the door hook but on its own hanger. Hand-wash your beloved knitwear pieces and douse your favourite booties in fabric guard before you expose them to the elements. That way, both you and your wardrobe will endure the chilliest winters year after year in indefatigable style.

Okay, lecture's over now.

6

ACCESSORIES

There isn't much a girl can't handle, provided she's armed with the right accessories. For me it's like candy for the body, the sweet treats that inspire a girlish excitement as you adorn yourself with your favourite ring, neck scarf, or daytime clutch.

When you're done with denim shopping or finished with the frock search, it's oh so easy and quite amazingly inexpensive to update your look and transform your mood with a handful of desirable adjuncts.

Like the icing on your best friend's birthday cake, or even the lighting of its candles, these pieces are usually applied last minute, yet deliver maximum aesthetic satisfaction.

Yes, they're non-essential—many women can ooze style in just a beautiful sweater and jeans—but wouldn't she look somehow unfinished? As with make-up, accessories are usually badly handled because women overdo them, or else neglect to wear them altogether.

For many of us, the application of these stylish trinkets is not instinctive, so I'm urging you here to *make an effort*. As you're dressing, don't just throw on clothes and run, think about what pieces you own that might lift the outfit, like a scarf, a glamorous pair of earrings, or alternative bag to the usual sack you cart around.

YET, THOSE WHO ARE GREEDY FOR NECKLACES, RINGS AND SCARVES MAY NEED TO HEED COCO CHANEL'S ADVICE ON THE MATTER, 'WHEN ACCESSORISING ALWAYS TAKE OFF THE LAST ITEM YOU PUT ON.'

I have stylish friends who adore covering themselves in jewellery, and others who adopt Chanel's more minimalist advice. Both look fabulous because they're keeping to their own personal tastes. Just don't try to make a statement with every aspect of your dress, handbag, shoes, and jewellery. Your look should be a balance between the bold bits and the simpler subtleties. Sounds daunting? Then read on.

Handbags and gladrags: how to harness your inner bag lady

Whatever your body size, whatever your colouring and wherever you live, a beautiful handbag will make any woman feel spectacular. Handbags are a girl's best friend because they personalize our outfits, perhaps more than any other accessory. How else do you allow your t-shirt and jeans to really tell a story about *you*?

The genesis from pouch to slouchy tote has been a drama of feminist proportions, as we've witnessed women using their handbags to announce their power, state their personal style and, increasingly with the advent of the 'it-bag', to indicate their private wealth.

Don't be a (tw)it-bag

The 'it-bag' rose to power in the late 90s and is still a fashion phenomenon, which lurks in the shadows today. It typically denotes a high-end handbag, made by a luxurious label; they tend to be sported by few 'it' celebrities and consequentially coveted by millions. They sparked a movement away from the handbag figuring as an investment piece to carry you through decades, whole epochs of your stylish lifespan, and instead becoming an item of transitory trendiness. Hence, novelty is an essential factor to the 'it-bag'—many of which feature distinctive embellishments, such as graphical logos, sheepskin, padlocks, tassels, or chains. But this novelty led the handbag, wrongly I think, becoming a short shelf-life throwaway item, something that you seasonally spring-cleaned off your arm and out of your wardrobe.

Only a woman of stoic resolve can withstand this handbag hurricane without getting caught up in a twister and devouring those fashion magazines, which can coerce you into the cult, into hankering for a new handbag season after season.

A STYLISH WOMAN SHOULD NEVER BE A SLAVE TO CULTISH TRENDS OR 'IT' BRANDS. SHE TENDS TO FIND A FEW DESIGNERS WHOSE ACCESSORIES WORK WITH HER AESTHETIC AND STICKS TO THEIR SIDE LIKE A LOYAL LABRADOR.

But how and when to invest?

Avoid falling into the 'it-bag' trap, which will date very quickly, by prizing quality and workmanship over quirky, faddish details. Choose a distinctive shape that is practical and capacious, a timeless design which will last you decades, like a good piece of furniture.

SMART AND STYLISH GIRLS ARE ALWAYS ON THE LOOKOUT FOR EMERGING ACCESSORY DESIGNERS, ESPECIALLY IF THEY TRAVEL ABROAD. HERE YOU CAN PICK UP BEAUTIFUL PIECES BY LESSER KNOWN BRANDS WHICH MAY IN THE FUTURE WORK OUT TO BE A SMART INVESTMENT, LIKE AN ENTERPRISING ART COLLECTOR.

Your bag may not have the cultish kudos of the moment, but if it's truly beautiful and well-designed, in the long run you will get greater, and more subtle, style mileage.

Spending a sizeable sum of money on a luxurious handbag is an investment which, in my opinion, requires no defence. A beautiful bag is a truly transformative accessory with the capacity to work magic on both your outfit and sartorial spirit. This is no more evident than in the professional sphere, where a handbag can figure as a powerful emblem, a subtle weapon wielded by women which announces their refinement, independence and insistence on quality.

TO MAKE A GOOD INVESTMENT, WHATEVER YOUR PRICE BRACKET, YOUR DAY BAG NEEDS TO BE A VERSATILE COLOUR.

You may be full of organized intentions, of changing your bag each day to coordinate with your outfit, but in reality such occasions are scarce, na? You end up leaving something important in yesterday's bag and cursing your caprice for the rest of the day.

TO BE SAFE, OPT FOR SOMETHING IN BLACK OR A TAN SHADE WHICH GOES WITH EVERYTHING. METALLICS AND ANIMAL SKINS CAN ALSO BE SURPRISINGLY FLEXIBLE OPTIONS, IF YOU WANT TO BREAK OUT OF BLACK AND BROWN.

Indulging in a sumptuous skin such as ostrich, crocodile, alligator, or python will seem excessive when you initially sign the dotted line, but these leathers last for generations and can oscillate between casual and eveningwear as the occasion demands.

Stylish contents: be sure to carry fattering clutter

Your day bag needs to be big enough to carry around the countless weird and wonderful items that a handbag should contain. Mary Poppins managed to bewitch her carpet holdall into carrying a coat stand and umbrella amongst her bits and pieces, but that's perhaps a bit extreme. To be suitably capacious, your bag needs the following essential items to keep you looking and feeling stylish throughout the day.

- Phone (possibly two)
- Wallet (often a large piece in itself)

- Keys
- Diary
- Sunglasses
- Make-up (including tinted lip balm, blusher, and mascara)
- Compact mirror (for those after dinner, spinach-in-teeth concerns)
- Chewing gum or mint (see above)
- Small bottle of perfume
- Book, kindle, or iPad (for traffic jams and delayed departures)

Other helpful bits of handbag weaponry include a hairbrush, hand cream, facial mist. Essential for the morning after the night before. Of course, if you've entered into early motherhood then your bag will need to be triple this size in order to contain the relevant infant paraphernalia of nappies and wipes. But don't fear, you do not have to resort to ugly, wipe-clean nappy bags. Many tote holdalls are large enough now to contain all the essentials.

Size wise

It may come as a surprise to some of you but a handbag is as much of a vital component of your outfit to consider when you're dressing for your body size as a bra or waist belt. It's important not to let your everyday bag weigh you down or overwhelm you. Clear it out regularly otherwise you'll end up toting around a sack of Santa Claus proportions, risking scoliosis or else the silhouette of the man in red himself.

IF YOU'RE PARTICULARLY CURVY, BE AWARE THAT A LARGE, UN-SCULPTED BAG CAN ADD A LEVEL OF BULK TO YOUR FRAME THAT YOU COULD DO WITHOUT. WIDE BOTTOMED, RECTANGULAR BAGS CAN ALSO HAVE A WIDENING EFFECT ON YOUR HIPS AND STOMACH, SO TREAD CAREFULLY THERE.

A messenger bag or a luxurious leather satchel, can emphasize the waist and work wonders for curvy girls—just don't let it rest too far down on your hips. But if you're pear-shaped then remember that a cross-body bag can work as a flashing arrow to your lower half pointing out your worst features!

SIMILARLY, THOSE WHO ARE NOTICEABLY BUXOM UP TOP SHOULD STEER CLEAR OF CROSS-BODY BAGS—THE STRAP CAN ACT AS A BIZARRE PARTITION BETWEEN RIGHT AND LEFT BREAST.

Sharp framed and willowy framed girls should opt for slouchier, long handled handbags to soften your silhouette and play up to your graceful, supermodel stature.

Petite girls have to pay careful attention to proportion. Do not succumb to the temptation of channelling those stick-thin celebrities who sport oversized it-bags like colonic sacks—it's a clown-like trend best left at the turn of the millennium.

HOLD YOUR HANDBAG AGAINST AND IN FRONT OF YOUR BODY IN THE MIRROR— IS IT WIDER THAN YOU?

IF YES, YOU SHOULD CHOOSE SOMETHING SCALED DOWN THAT WON'T OVERWHELM YOUR FIGURE.

If you like wearing your bag across your body then a good trick is to try and buy one with adjustable straps, so you can experiment with the length and ensure it doesn't shorten your legs and rests against the slimmest part of your body.

I love Celine and Hermès handbags because they occupy a great position between laid-back style and lady-like chic. The slightly rigid shape gives you a chic outline but the long bodystrap and capacious size make them perfect for the daytime.

> There's no excuse for carrying your laptop in a dowdy bag. Treat your trusted technology with the respect it deserves and invest in a beautiful case. Your local market will offer lots of cheap styles but I love Smythson and Nappa Dori.

Ah, the clutch

Its definitive lack of handles is what makes this item such a stylish accessory, granting instant chic to whoever sports one. By overcoming the inherent impracticality of a bag without hurdles the wearer immediately ascends to a divinely stylish realm; she is personalizing her outfit and making a stylish statement rather than succumbing to the bonds of practicality. Who needs hands anyway?

❖ The evening clutch

Investing in a beautiful evening clutch bag that you love will set your heart racing and can guarantee all-night smugness, whoever you're meeting and however bad your evening is.

If you're wearing Indian clothes then I recommend keeping your accessories traditional to complete the look. The batwa is such a timeless piece, so be sure to check out your Mum's collection before buying anything. If you are purchasing a new one, then pick a useful metallic shade like champagne; or opt for the dominant colour from the pattern on your sari. Whenever my Mum had a new sari tailored she'd always make a batwa with the leftover material, which I think is a great trick as you then have a ready-made complete accessory to work with each outfit!

If you're moving away from the traditional styles, then you have a huge range of options available to you. Unfortunately, few of these feature that useful little handle, so you'll have to learn how to balance your drink and clutch bag without losing either of them. (Clue: work on armpit grip.)

THE KEY TO SPORTING THE RIGHT CLUTCH HAS LITTLE TO DO WITH MATERIAL OR COLOUR BUT EVERYTHING TO DO WITH SIZE.

In your mind's eye, create a sliding scale for the formality of your evening event. The more formal the occasion, the smaller your bag should be (but never smaller than the size of your hand!). On these occasions you must also enlist a chaperone with pockets for the purveyance of those larger, equally crucial props for your evening. Invitations, hairbrushes, phones, etc., are best left in a partner's capacious pocket to keep your dinky clutch looking perfect.

Where a sangeet or formal birthday party would require a smaller, more understated clutch, drinks in a bar, dinner at a restaurant or a house party call demand what

I call your 'party clutch'. Here you can have so much fun with colour, material, and embellishment to transform a neutral outfit into a talking point, something really personal and unique.

YOUR PARTY CLUTCH IS ALSO THE PERFECT WAY TO ADD AN ACCENT INTO YOUR OUTFIT WITHOUT GOING THE WHOLE WAY, SO DON'T SHY FROM ANIMAL PRINTS, NEONS, OR EVEN PERSPEX MATERIALS IF THEY TAKE YOUR FANCY.

The day clutch

Clutch bags used to be one of the few pieces of fashion which comprised the fabric of our style cosmology and divided night and day. The handbag was diurnal, the clutch nocturnal. But recently a new breed has arrived on the party scene: the day clutch—a larger sized, less sparkly version of the original intended for 24-hour usage.

I think this can be an enormously powerful style statement, provided the context is correct. A day clutch taken shopping will leave you feeling frustrated and incapacitated; at the airport it's unthinkable. Yet wielding an envelope clutch in the office, or at a power lunch will, like a good ponytail, give an unexpected burst of satisfaction and stylish swishi-ness. Keep your clutch capacious (tiny day clutches are a style tautology) and restrict yourself to matte tones to ensure your look stays appropriate and polished.

TEAM WITH:

- trouser suits for an immaculate androgenous look
- full 50s skirts and a crisp white shirt

WHERE TO BUY?

Shopping for your perfect handbag is an intensely personal process that must not be rushed. Research online to refine your tastes and avoid instances of impulsive, mustard-yellow purchases. Both netaporter.com and mywardrobe.com allow you to search for styles by colour and designer.

If you're buying non-labelled items then you should still insist on leather—it will last so much longer and I've known plastic handbags to melt in summer months. Whilst bagging yourself cheaper street imitations of luxury bags is stylishly savvy; sporting a designer knock-off or fake is not. It suggests slavishness to branding without the bank balance to back it up—in short, a little bit designer desperate.

Best in Class

Classic designs: Hermès, Chanel, Prada, Louis Vuitton, Giorgio Armani
Slouchy shape: Marc Jacobs, Mulberry, Rara Avis, Stella McCartney
Clutch bags: Lovetobag, Miu Miu, Sanya V Jain, Karishma Saerna, VBH
Experimental: Corto Moltedo, Tom Ford, Chan Olympia

Luxe for Less

Classic designs: Zara, Mango
Slouchy shape: Forever 21, Accessorize, Yashwant Market in Delhi
Clutch bags: Topshop
Experimental: TopShop

Sunglasses: the importance of being shaded

We all know the frequently lauded benefits of protecting your twinkling peepers, but in reality there's much more to sunglasses than meets the eye.

Break up, hangover, walk of shame, 12-hour flight, court date: these miraculous winged lenses will add instant camouflage, helping you glide effortlessly through all the most difficult situations in modern life. So my non-negotiable advice is to remain constantly within three feet of your favourite pair.

From Jackie O to Sharmilla Tagore, sunglasses have been synonymous with style, but why? I think it's because they protect your privacy and create a layer of impenetrable cool between you and your scores of admirers.

COVERING YOUR EYES IS A WAY OF RISING ABOVE THE USUAL PHYSICAL INTERACTION DEMANDED OF EVERYDAY HUMAN BEINGS; IT'S AN ACCESSORY WHICH SPELLS 'DO NOT DISTURB' MORE THAN ANY OTHER.

Take care, however, with this accessory, not to appear too inaccessible. Few fashionistas can work the sunglasses-inside-even-if-it's-pretty-dark formula. Anna Wintour is famous for sporting her frames in the front row at fashion weeks, appearing unfussed by the array of beautiful items sashaying down the catwalk, but for the rest of us the overall effect can be cliché ice queen rather than approachable.

REMEMBER THAT, WITH ENOUGH SLEEP, YOUR EYES WILL BE YOUR MOST SPARKLING FEATURE, SO DON'T KEEP THEM PERMANENTLY COVERED!

Sunglasses are an amazing tool for accenting a plain outfit (see **Chapter 7: Accenting**) and introducing an added dimension of to your look, like preppy, retro, or downright outrageous.

My favourite pair at the moment are my precious cat-eye frames from Cutler and Gross because the frames and lenses are black they go with everything, and I love how they inject a slice of Audrey Hepburn, retro glamour into my daily outfits.

Perhaps more than any other accessory, sunglasses are made for experimenting and fun. Beware of investing, as with it-bags, into faddy frames which will date very quickly. Does anyone remember those ubiquitous Chloe frames with the diamante hearts? You're lucky if not—we'd probably all sooner forget those now. Retro styles can look amazingly classic yet original, so keep your eyes open in any second-hand markets for aviator or wayfarer frames (or your grandparents' closet for that matter).

Shopping for sunglasses is an intensely personal activity, but I would advise you to take a friend whose opinion you can trust. The styles out there are innumerable and colours countless, which we should be grateful for, because it can be excruciatingly difficult to find a pair to suit your face.

Oval

Key features: balanced forehead, cheekbones, and jaw.

Lucky oval-faced girls can get away with a range of styles, so long as you pay attention to proportions. Look for softly angular frames which will emphasize the symmetrical contours.

Heart-shaped

Key features: wide forehead and cheekbones; narrow chin.

Heart-shaped faces need to look for styles which won't emphasize the width of the forehead or the slight imbalance in the lower part of your face. Steer clear of thick frames and opt for something more delicate. Feel free to try larger lenses but ensure they don't sit too high; choose something like a 70s style in a wire frame, which will bring the attention to your face downwards.

Round

It's important to look for frames with straight or angular lines that will lengthen and slim the face and add definition. Avoid rounded styles that accentuate full cheeks.

Square

Key features: broad forehead; square jawline.

Square-faced girls will usually look amazing in oversized frames with round lenses (while the rest of us risk looking like ants). Draw attention away from your jawline by looking for frames which will sit slightly higher on your cheekbones.

Five classic styles and how to wear them

1) 70s style

The look: Large, square frames with graduated lenses. Think Diane Keaton in *Annie Hall*.

Are they for me? Round, heart, and oval faces work brilliantly with this enduring style.

Team with: Maxi dresses or palazzo pants with a slouchy bag for a boho-luxe look

2) Aviators

The look: Unisex, classic shape with reflective or graduated lenses. Can be double framed at top. Think Tom Cruise in *Top Gun*.

Are they for me? Delicate frames work best with heart-shaped faces; rounder and square features benefit from their distinctly angular shape.

Team with: Casual combinations such as denim shorts, converse, and t-shirts. But you can also get creative and team yours with smarter outfits, such as a floral dress and fitted blazer.

3) Cat eyes

The look: Think Audrey Hepurn or Stanley Kubrick's *Lolita*. These frames often have a dramatic flare to the outer corner of the eye or the swoop can be more subtle. Look out for pretty embellished frames if you're feeling brave.

Are they for me? Square and oval-faced beauties looking to make a distinctly feminine impression. Professional women complete their work outfits with these neat and classic frames.

Team with: Monochrome outfits, especially your little black dress, can look ultra-dramatic with these shades. Don't forget a string of pearls to complete your *Breakfast at Tiffany's* look.

4) Oversized

The look: Jackie O, Victoria Beckham, Anna Wintour

Are they for me? The square faced among us suit these well, providing they have the glamorous attitude to pull them off.

Team with: A celebrity swagger and statement handbag. Ensure you're looking polished enough to pull off the bombast of this style and accessorize with a smile to avoid looking too ice-queen.

5) Wayfarers

The look: The best-selling sunglasses in all of history, angular yet rounded, suiting men and women of all ages. Deliciously donned by Edward Cullen in *Twilight*. Look out for 80s clubmaster styles which feature lenses with a half-rim—equally elegant.

Are they for me? Hooray for this ubiquitous and all-forgiving style! Wayfarers look good on just about anyone.

Team with: The subtle masculinity of these shades give an edge to preppy and girlie outfits, but complement your punkier pieces just as beautifully. Stick to classic colours unless you're at a rave or music festival.

Jewellery

'You can't cry on a diamond's shoulder, and diamonds won't keep you warm at night, but they're sure fun when the sun shines'—**Elizabeth Taylor**

Just like underwear, jewellery is one of those things that you have to remember to put on before you leave the house. Don't get lazy and neglect its transformative powers, you'll end up stepping out like a dowdy hedge when you could dazzle like a Christmas tree.

BUT EQUALLY, BEWARE OF YOUR INDIVIDUAL TENDENCY TO SHED JEWELLERY—DON'T WEAR PIECES WHICH YOU'LL INEVITABLY DISCARD THROUGHOUT THE DAY—I'VE LOST COUNTLESS BANGLES THROUGH LAPTOP USAGE, PEELING OFF LAYERS, AND WASHING HANDS.

How much jewellery to wear at a given moment is a matter down to personal taste; the much debated question is as long as a string of pearls. French women say you should never wear a necklace and earrings both, for risk of looking too *gauche*. We Indian women prefer ourselves slightly more adorned (understatement), and can look amazing in bangles and complete jewellery sets, which is absolutely right because we started it! One of the first civilizations to start making jewellery were the peoples of the Indus Valley (now Pakistan and Punjab) and we were the first country to mine diamonds. It's only natural that as a nation we are obsessed, and that we should want to adorn ourselves in the fruits of our region!

Great jewellery can and should be a talking piece, (see: 'meeting the parents') and will hold greater sentimental value than any item in your wardrobe. Let it reflect you and your history, your travels, and family. Please do not follow 'must-have jewellery trends' which urge you to invest in this season's must-have gem such as agate or coral. Beautiful as both materials are, your collection should be a gradual collation over the years, rather than a smash and grab in Accessorize or Forever 21.

Which brings me to my next ring in the chain.

FINE JEWELLERY DOESN'T NECESSARILY HAVE TO BE IN-FINE-ITELY EXPENSIVE.

My advice would be to practice on costume jewellery before you give into the gem-tation and invest (or enchant your partner enough to treat you). That way you will know for certain which colours and styles suit you best before you splurge. One tip for successfully persuading everyone your costume jewellery is Cartier is to remember that the larger the stone, the less real it looks. So if you're aiming to maintain the guise of a rich, dazzling Indian lady without faltering, then limit your gem dimensions to something more subtle.

While I can't tell you how much to wear at any one time (I have one lawyer friend who adorns every part of her body constantly and looks incredible), there is a Libran balance to be struck when matching your clothes with your gleaming gems. Essentially, if your jewellery is bold, bombastic and beautiful, let your clothes take a back seat and keep them simple. Likewise, if you're pushing boundaries in a one shoulder leopard print playsuit with sequinned stilettos, it's probably best to keep your jewellery muted and uncomplicated.

DON'T ALLOW YOUR JEWELLERY TO COMPETE WITH ONE ANOTHER.

If you're attending a wedding then opt for a set—it's an easy way to ensure everything will work together in harmony. Likewise, a statement cocktail ring should trump anything else, so don't try and impose coloured necklaces or complicated earrings when your hand can speak for itself.

Before I go into detail over necklace lengths, earring drops and the perfect number of bangles, there are a few pieces of jewellery which should form the inner crust of every stylish woman's coffer.

Essential items for your jewellery wardrobe

'Bags of fiery opals, sapphires, amethysts,
Jacinths, hard topaz, grass-green emeralds,
Beauteous rubies, sparkling diamonds...'
—**Christopher Marlowe**

Studs

One pair of stud earrings is essential to take you all the way from breakfast to bleary-eyed cab home in style. Think creatively here; they don't have to be simple gold or pearl. Go for a coloured stone or larger-than-lobe shape to perk up your daily outfits. Wear with your hair in a demi-chignon or open to maximize the subtle appeal of your favourite pair.

Cuffs and bangles

Because sleeves are simply not enough. Wrists are one of the most underrated and sexy parts of a woman's body. Play up to your coquettish strengths and adorn your wrists in something lovely. I will love bangles until the end of time; they can inject an essential dose of colour into your LBD, and it's so much fun to experiment with their textures, such as pairing a knotted or embellished gold bangle with a host of glass janglies. If you're looking to try something different, then try a sculpted embellished cuff to update your look.

Cocktail rings

Your chunky ring is an essential mood lift, and a great way to dress up a plain party dress. If your outfit is particularly busy and high-necked then accessorize at arm's length rather than confusing glitters with earrings and necklaces. I love styles such as those designed by Amaya and Bansi (Pernia's Pop-Up Shop), but you can also pick up some blinging cocktail pieces in Accessorize. Derive eternal pleasure and love from your rings by getting creative—stack your chunky cocktail ring with your minimalist bands to make a bolder statement.

ALWAYS, ALWAYS GIVE YOURSELF A MANICURE BEFORE PLACING YOUR CHUNKY RING ON THAT FINGER. NEGLECT THAT GOLDEN RULE (I DON'T HAVE MANY!) AND IT'S LIKE ASKING SOMEONE TO VIEW YOUR FLAT AFTER AN ALL-NIGHT PARTY OR HECTIC WEEK AT WORK—TOTALLY INADMISSIBLE AND ULTRA UNSTYLISH.

Hoops

I love hoops because they frame your face beautifully and are so versatile. Encrusted pairs can add texture and funk to a simple tube dress, while a smaller gold pair will add feminine glamour to a white shirt at work. If you want to showcase something stand out, then wear your hair up, and keep your make-up classic and classy to avoid overkill. Not to be worn if you're in possession of a grabby infant.

Chandelier and jhumka earrings

If you want to invest in fine jewellery, then a pair of ornate chandelier or jhumka earrings will be your smartest move. They are the obvious choice for formal events, but can win you surprise style points if you pair them with a vest top and jeans—so unexpectedly luxe! When browsing, keep in mind the length of your neck. You should have at least one and half inches between the end of the necklace and the top of your shoulder; and more if your neck is shorter than average. If your face is round, then a narrow style will lengthen your proportions and keep you looking sleek. When your ears are making a bold statement, then it's generally advisable to keep the neck naked or minimally decorated. That said, if you instinctively want to wear more, and your outfit is plain, then don't suppress the urge but do consider your reflection carefully.

OVER-ACCESSORISING CAN BE A POWERFUL STYLE STATEMENT, BUT IT WORKS ONLY FOR THOSE WHO JANGLE WITH UNCHALLENGEABLE CONFIDENCE.

Long layered necklaces

A long layered necklace with an interesting pendant can transfigure an outfit from dowdy to bohemian in one swoop. It will also work wonders for your body shape by lengthening the torso and drawing the eye downwards. There's no secret in the layering, you just throw it over your regular necklace and keep it tucked outside of your clothes.

KEEP THE CHAIN MINIMAL AND IN SILVER OR GOLD, BUT EXPERIMENT WITH YOUR PENDANT.

I love pieces by Eina Ahluwalia but you can find amazing charms wherever you look; it's up to you to choose something that reflects your personality. That said, avoid anything too gimmicky, tacky hearts or plastic charms can look a little cheap and immature.

Short delicate necklaces

This should be something that you sleep in. Invest wisely in this and you'll only require one or two in your lifetime. This piece should fall at what's known as the 'princess length'—17 to 19 inches and just below your throat. It should be plain enough to layer easily with your longer necklace, but pretty enough to wear alone.

Statement necklaces

A statement necklace is your fall-back flair on cloudier days. Push yourself out of the comfortable confines of metallic shades and experiment with an array of glittering colours to make maximum impact.

These pieces are best worn with your plainer outfits; with black jeans and a crisp button down white shirt a statement necklace will help you ooze laid-back luxury.

Keep proportions in mind here; don't swamp your petite neck with anything too heavy. Avoid the temptation to continue the statement from your ear lobes; keep the rest of your jewellery minimal and let your neck do the talking.

NECKLACES: HOW LOW DO YOU GO?

Have you ever seen someone totally glammed-up, and in theory amazing, but something seems just a little bit off? Wearing the wrong necklace length with a given neckline is a common jewellery-error that women make. So consider the following guidelines before you step out:

- Chokers rest perfectly at the base of the neck, and look ultra-stylish with strapless or plunging necklines. These work best for girls with graceful, swan-like necks.

- Collar necklaces should lie snugly around the middle of the neck, and can be worn with V-neck, boat-neck, and off-the-shoulder tops.
- Princess length necklaces (17 to 19 inches) are the most common and versatile necklace length and should fall just below the throat. They work with most necklines except anything too high.
- Matinee length necklaces (20 to 24 inches) hit the top of the bust, so I wouldn't recommend wearing this length with cleavage plunging outfits. If the necklace hits the very top of your neckline, it won't rest properly.
- Opera length necklaces (28 to 34 inches) fall below the bust and look great with a very high neckline or an average V-neck. This is where your layering necklace comes into play, so have fun and double up a few for a cute daytime look.

Be age-appropriate

'Jewelry takes people's minds off your wrinkles'

—**Sonja Henie**

20–40+

Pearls might be your best friend during this age, but they can also age you dramatically. Capitalize on their opalescence, which flatters almost all skin tones, by opting for a pearl hoop, or perhaps a drop, rather than a traditional necklace or studs, which can look a little frumpy. Otherwise, this is the period when you should start collating your collection. Begin by raiding your mum and grandma's collection (with permission!), then make use of your wide travels to pick up original pieces.

50+

I think the older you get, the more adventurous you can become with jewellery. Ethnic, bolder pieces work beautifully for women over 50 who want to enhance slightly less fussy, refined clothing.

> **A STATEMENT 'SOMETHING' ABOUT THE NECK IS ALSO A GREAT WAY TO DIVERT ATTENTION AWAY FROM A 'CREPEY' AREA.**

Whether your amazing Masai necklace was sourced on an actual trip you've made, or actually was a wise investment, is anyone's guess at this age. Carefully chosen pieces can add mystique, allure, and a sense of history—crucially without dating you.

Unfortunately, the older you are, the harder it is to get away with shiny, cheaper things. Like a lioness with her pride, you should preside proudly over your collection and only showcase the quality pieces of enduring beauty.

Scarves to the rescue

I bow down in reverence to the Hermès scarf. While not a wardrobe staple, it is a style classic to be handed down through generations, wickedly sourced in vintage shops at bargain prices or gifted to your closest girlfriend as if a baton in a beautiful relay race founded on style and femininity. Too much? I don't think so; these scarves are woven from the silk of 250 mulberry moth cocoons, they deserve a bit of respect!

Of course, mulberry moth cocoons demand a hefty price tag, and you don't have to invest here.

SILK SCARVES ARE TOTALLY UBIQUITOUS AND YOU CAN EASILY PICK UP BEAUTIFUL PIECES AT A MUCH LOWER PRICE. BUT IF IT'S GOOD ENOUGH FOR GRACE KELLY AND QUEEN ELIZABETH, THEN SURELY IT'S A LUXURY YOU DESERVE, NA?

How do I wear mine? Let me count the ways...

The adjustable tie

Arrange your scarf around your neck and create a knot on one side. Loop the other half through and adjust length so that the knot falls at the top of your cleavage line. For added creative style points, take one of your statement cuff bracelets or a brooch and fix it to the knot.

The pussy bow

Fold the scarf into a strip, tie a knot at the end of one side and slip the other side through the knot and you have yourself a cute little bowtie! Perfect this technique and you'll be power dressing in seconds.

The infinity

Take the two ends of your scarf and tie them into double knots. Then double your loop over your head twice or thrice until your neck is wrapped up and snug. Make sure you adjust and hide the seams to make them invisible.

The robe

Arrange your scarf equally around your neck and flatten it out against your body. Take a waist belt and belt the pieces in place. Alternatively, drape the scarf into a kimono shape over your shoulders and belt in place. Your silhouette will now be totally elegant.

The waterfall

Double loop your scarf around your neck and with the corner of one side which is nearest to you, tuck it into the neck. Open out the folds so that they drape down over your torso like a gentle cascade. Ahhh!

...and that's just worn at the neck! I fix mine on my ponytail, wear it as a bow headband, create a turban out of it to wear on the beach, as a belt, or tie it as a cute-preppy accent on an old leather bag. Unleash your creativity—there are no bounds to the different ways you can wear these, though perhaps limit yourself at bib.

WHERE TO BUY?

Best in class: Hermès, Ekaya (Pernia's Pop-Up Shop), Pooja Aggarwal (Pernia's Pop-Up Shop)

Cheap n chic: Forever 21, Zara, Vintage Shops, Sarojini Nagar market

7

ACCENTING

No, I'm not talking about the ability to pull off ze chiccest French aczent with aplomb. Style accenting actually relates to trends: the small or minor ways a dominant trend becomes incorporated into your daily wardrobe. Up until this point I've preached ultimate caution in loading your shopping basket with the latest trends to appear down the catwalks or in fashion magazines. But we don't live in a fashion-vacuum, and the chances are you're going to be seduced by many seasonal styles that appear temptingly on the streets, in movies, and online.

Personal authenticity is the key to channelling trends and avoiding looking like a fashion victim. Is the leopard-look not quite you? Then leave animal print alone, even if it's threatening you from every angle. The authentic-approach is of paramount importance, because it's the only way to ensure you maintain your own style identity.

With the right accents introduced into your basic clothing combinations, you'll still look like you, but just a little more of-the-moment.

Neon

It was acceptable in the 80s, but it's just as fabulous today. And I totally understand why! Neon is such a fizzy and fun use of colour, guaranteed to lift your mood and make your heart pop. Of course, as with all accents, neon should be introduced in fragments. It's very important to keep in mind the background palate for your neon performance: for daytime I think camel and white tones work better with neons than black—they keep the look fresh without too harsh a contrast.

TAKE YOUR FIRST TENTATIVE STEPS BY TEAMING A MINTY FRESH GREEN NAIL POLISH WITH A GOOD NEUTRAL, SUCH AS A FLOATY WHITE DRESS.

Ensure you opt for the correct tone of neon for your skin colour. Fuschia pinks and oranges will work beautifully on Indian skin tones. For a neon accent worn further away from your face, a skinny belt tied at the waist will break up the dull colour and bring all the attention to the slimmest part of your body—good work!

POP TIPS FOR NEON!

- Remember, wearing neon is a little like taking a highlighter to one part of your body—so ensure it's something you want to stand out.
- In general, be wary of neon on the lower half of your body. Opt for something like an acid green mini skirt with a baggy white t-shirt over fuschia leggings or trousers—these are much harder to pull off.
- If you want to make a full neon-announcement, say with a bright mini-dress, then maintain a simple colour contrast and don't confuse your overall statement. Team with nude shoes, a metallic clutch, and a siren attitude.
- A silk scarf in bright neon is an elegant and modern way to update your grey work suit, but if it's an interview then opt for something safer.
- Matching neon-jewellery is generally unadvisable. Keep neon jewellery to one statement only.
- I say this rarely, and don't enjoy preaching it, but neon clothing is, in general, a younger trend. Over 50s should channel this with accessories or nails only.

Fashion Dictionary

Chartreuse: Term liberally thrown around by fashion types when discussing neon colour palates, but true meaning and etymology understood by few. Term denotes that specific shade which rests between yellow and green, and stems from delicious French liqueur of the same colour concocted by Carthusian monks in 1732. Magnifique!

WHERE TO BUY?

Best in class: Christopher Kane, Masaba, Tresor, Valliyan

Cheap n chic: Forever 21

Animal prints

How to tame your inner leopard-o-holic

Maybe it's the Pakistani in me, but I just can't run away from animal prints. A leopard never changes his spots, just as animal print will never go out of fashion. Fierce and predatory, inherently sensual and strong, the print is both timeless and cross-generational.

There's something so instinctive about wearing animal designs, the sense that we are refashioning the most stylish animals that stalk this earth.

AS LEOPARD PRINT-PIONEER, THE WONDERFUL ROBERTO CAVALLI SAYS, 'IT'S LIKE COPYING THE NATURE THAT GOD CREATED.'

I wholeheartedly believe that there is no occasion in any stylish woman's calendar which would not benefit from even a tail-swish of animal print. It's a myth that it only works for the more garishly styled among us. In fact, it's a wardrobe staple to such an extent that I also believe, given the right gradation, leopard or tiger prints can figure as a neutral tone to wear alongside your brighter pieces.

But how to channel your inner tigress over barbaric cavewoman?

It is not uncommon that women fall in love with this addictive textile so devotedly that they are unable to stop wearing it. How to spot this in your friends? Their world becomes one large hunting lodge, crafted from leopard-print handbags, stilettos, nail art, phone covers, and even bedspreads. They openly suggest that Cruella de Vil should have made this year's most stylish list. The purr when they talk. Once addiction takes hold, it's unlikely that you will be able to recognize these symptoms in yourself—it's unfortunately more unlikely that a friend will stage an intervention. So my advice is, as ever, to surround yourself with honest friends who love you and will tell you when you look ridiculous.

But how much is too much?

Overdoing leopard print isn't always a simple case of numbers but a matter of *balancing tones*.

It's often preached against, but I think some women can get away with exhibiting a herd of different animal prints together in one outfit by mixing different gradations and tones. For example, a silky black blouse with subtle leopard printing tucked into a grey snakeskin pencil skirt can look extraordinarily powerful and fashion-forward.

It's also so much fun to experiment, and pair a strong leopard print with an equally bold colour, such as emerald green. If you're heading in this direction, just remember to keep the palate limited to print + colour (including shoes) and ensure the colour you're using is suitably rich-looking and not too gaudy (for example, red can be risky).

Personally, I prefer to use animal print in accents and accessories such as a leopard-print cardigan. I have a pair of incredible Louboutin leopard Oxford pumps which are extremely alluring, but I always wear them with something simple, like jeans, to tone them down. Likewise, if you're going for an ultra bold leopard-print dress and you feel a little self conscious, balance the tone with a black cardigan rather than sequined jacket. Camel works just as well as a balancing tone here if you feel the contrast with black is too harsh.

As well as balancing the tones in your outfit, it's equally important to identify the best tone of animal print that works for your colouring. Most Indian skin tones work extremely well with darker-based, more muted animal prints, and we can pull off tiger print perhaps better than any other nationality (naturally!). Paler girls in grey snakeskin risk looking washed out, while brassy blondes risk looking cheap in brighter prints.

ANIMAL PRINT MATHEMATICS

- Leopard print blouse + red lipstick + sleek bun = second date sexual predator
- White floaty dress + animal print scarf + boho hair = flirty feline
- Animal print dress + thick black opaque tights + black ballet flats = furry winter warmth
- Snakeskin blouse + white jeans + Oxford pumps = venomously stylish

Beware: animal print traps!

- Neon or artificially-coloured animal print—aside from black and white—authentic camouflage is key.
- Any garment which uses an animal print background, then embellished with flowers, or worse, logos.
- Animal print will reveal an inner feline—so don't overplay its seductive subtlety.

WHERE TO BUY?

Best in class: Roberto Cavalli

Cheap n chic: H&M

Masculine—if I were a boy...

The little black tux was Yves Saint Laurent's prodigal first foray into the world of androgyny. His infamous 'Le Smoking' jacket reinvented the fashion community's ideals of femininity and produced the ultimate adversary to the LBD. It scandalized some, but was coveted by many. Today, YSL is credited for putting trousers into the wardrobes of women, and making all of our lives a little bit more comfortable.

But how to capture the recurring trend for androgyny if your usual look is ultra-feminine?

MY FIRST PIECE OF ADVICE HERE IS SIMPLY TO TRY IT IN THE FIRST PLACE, EVEN IF IT'S JUST IN FRONT OF THE MIRROR AT HOME.

It might seem odd, especially since Indian women are so pre-conditioned to dress according to our chromosomes. But once you experience the strangely sultry sensation of donning a tuxedo, fedora hat or even a tie, you just might like it.

Androgynous accents are a sophisticated style move, which can be truly liberating when applied with conviction. But, like many of our accents, they depend on striking a balance between masculine and feminine, between harder and soft edged pieces. YSL's original tuxedo was softened with dramatic frilly cuffs and satin lapels, and you should follow suit. Introducing this duality may be something as simple as wearing your hair open, or donning a statement necklace or lipstick. You can emphasize the contrast even further and pair a floaty, feminine maxi skirt with a tuxedo jacket and blouse buttoned to the neck.

Boyfriend blazer and brogues

Le Smoking tuxedo of YSL is known elsewhere as the boyfriend blazer, and this is one important accent to harness when incorporating this trend into your wardrobe. Oversized in essence, but not to the extent that it swamps you, the key to a good boyf-blazer is the length—it should fall to the same place on your body as your boyfriend's suit jackets. Expect shoulders to be slightly looser than normal but the sleeves must fit your arms perfectly. There are some heavenly 80s-style boyfriend blazers out there in pastel-pinks and creams, if you still want to keep things girly.

Much loved by Sonam Kapoor, brogues are a flat lace-up shoe typically modelled on upstanding gentlemen. Yet you can also ooze gamine charm in an adorable short dress and these practical flats.

STEER CLEAR OF ANYTHING TOO CHUNKY FOR YOUR LEG SHAPE, UNLESS YOU WANT TO LOOK LIKE YOU'VE RAIDED YOUR GRANDFATHER'S CLOSET.

I think that's about all we can ransack from the closets of our male friends now ladies, so back to our own territory...

TIPS

Bianca Jagger famously went bare-chested when she wore her tuxedo suit...are you man enough? If not...try a beautiful bra or midriff-grazing cropped top or a sexy camisole

- Wear trousers to an event where you can second-guess the hemlines on your fellow females. So long as they're formal enough, why shouldn't you?
- No matter how masculine you're going, it's always advisable to wear a slick of make-up.
- Mismatched colours will break up a classic trouser suit for the daytime—try a peach blazer with brown tailored pants.
- Team your brogues with ankle socks to walk the line between dashing and dainty.
- Roll up the sleeves on your blazer to draw attention to your oh-so-fragile feminine wrists.

BOYFRIEND BLAZER MATHEMATICS

Boyfriend blazer + body-con dress + heeled booties = new romantic

Skinny jeans + striped shirt buttoned to neck + girly cardigan + brogues = schoolboy sweet

Boyfriend blazer + white t-shirt + tailored shorts + heels + envelope clutch = summer-city style crush

WHERE TO BUY?

Best in class: Stella McCartney, Nimish Shah (Pernia's Pop-Up Shop), Namrata Joshipura (Pernia's Pop-Up Shop)

Cheap n chic: Zara, Topshop

Leather

It was those brain-boxes at Celine who brought leather back to the fashion world's attention in 2010. Yet, for the mega-stylish among us, this wondrous fabric (if you can call it that, I prefer 'attitude') had never gone away.

Leather is a new-found obsession for because it's so versatile. It's allows you to look totally edgy but simultaneously sexy—there are remarkably few trend-accents which will grant you such instantaneous mystique and allure.

YOU DON'T HAVE TO BE A COMMITTED HELL'S ANGEL TO MAKE THE LEATHER TREND WORK

FOR YOU. IN FACT, THE EASIEST AND MOST VERSATILE WAY TO INCORPORATE LEATHER INTO YOUR DAILY WARDROBE IS WITH A JACKET.

You should spend time ensuring that you get the best cut for your body. Cropped and tightly fitted pieces are hugely popular at the moment, and I think they look great because they gently emphasize your waist and feminine frame. Don't dwarf yourself or bulk up your shoulders in anything too boxy and, if you can help it, steer clear of any leather jackets which are sneakily masquerading as other top half staples. I'm talking specifically about leather blazers here, or for that matter (shudder), leather trench-coats.

Leather jackets for your body shape

- **Narrow body**: Opt for something structured and double breasted—wear half zipped up to add width. An accentuated collar will also work wonders on your narrow shoulders and add a sense of drama to your look.

- **Big boobs**: Double breasted all the way—wear half zipped to keep your boobs liberated and your neck accentuated.

- **Broad shoulders/big bust**: You should seek out jackets with front detailing (be it studs, seams or stitches) which run down the middle of the jacket. This false contour will lead the eye away from the wider parts of your body. Tall, as well as broader ladies can look exquisite in a collarless jacket which will draw attention to your long and slim neck. Always try to find the lightest, most malleable leather, which will gently glide over your curves and soften your silhouette.

YES YOU CAN (WEAR LEATHER TROUSERS AND SKIRTS)!

If you want to move beyond the leather jacket then you're in luck, because designers are innovating. Where leather dresses, skirts and pants used to add inches in thickness and slow cook you from the inside, they've since moved onto designing leather pieces in much finer fabrics, with features appearing everywhere from handbags to t-shirts.

Leather skirts now come with flirty, soft leather flaring, allowing you to channel this repeat-trend in a more feminine way than ever before. Wear high on your waist and contrast with a tucked-in floaty blouses to capitalize on the power of polarities. This is also a wise piece for navigating between seasons; together with booties and a cropped knitted jumper (try an orange or cream) for winter and a sheer blouse, bare legs and flats for spring.

My personal leather uniform consists of a teeny black leather mini skirt from The Row, which I've practically slept in, and a pair of high-waisted leather pants from Balenciaga that you could also call my second skin. I love to wear both pieces with a tucked-in white t-shirt and eye-catching jewellery for a look which transports me from desk to a dinner date.

It came as an initial surprise to me that I was comfortable in leather trousers, since I consider myself much more of a Pink Lady than a T-Bird. Past polls have listed this much maligned item as the most regretted fashion purchase—but I'd wager opinions might have shifted with the recent advent of leather leggings.

A TIGHTER LEATHER PANT THAT WE'VE TRADITIONALLY SEEN IN THE PAST, LEATHER LEGGINGS MAKE A FABULOUS ALTERNATIVE TO DARK SKINNY JEANS, AND GIVE AN EVEN EDGIER EFFECT. I LOVE THE SLEEK SILHOUETTE THEY GIVE ME, AND THE FABULOUS WAY THE MATERIAL RUCHES AT THE FRONT TO GIVE A TEXTURED LOOK.

Depending on what you wear on your top half, these will work for most body shapes (pears should stick to leather skirts and dresses). Team with neutral shoes, a simple top, and let your legs make the style statement.

Leather mathematics

Leather mini skirt + blue blouse buttoned to top + simple chain + flats = casual correct!

Leather skinnies + cream lace top + coloured blazer + black Oxfords = sultry leather style

WHERE TO BUY?

Best in class: Acne, The Row, Balenciagga, Miu Miu

Cheap n chic: Zara, Topshop

Boho

Boho is the trend that downright refuses to drift away. Gypsies by nature—the word bohemian was used to describe travellers or refugees from central Europe—but you don't have to leave home to channel this trend with style. Each season we witness exciting new interpretations of this look on the catwalks, but beware—it's also a look which can be cringingly overdone.

FIRST OFF, YOU MUST REMEMBER THAT TO REMAIN AUTHENTIC, YOU MUST PAIR YOUR BOHO OUTFIT WITH A BREEZY ATTITUDE.

Run frantically for a bus in a hippie skirt, headband, and peace necklace and you'll appear more harassed hippie rather than free-spirited Goan godess.

As far as possible, the look needs to appear effortless. The key to this is using only a sprinkling of accents in any given outfit. There are few occasions when you can channel the entire look, such as music festivals and beach holidays, but for your urban existence I would keep the accents to three at maximum.

The bohemian trend has multiple spin-offs and sub-headings, but I have pinpointed its three main guises. Figure out which one best matches your personality and interpret its accents into your wardrobe whenever you feel in the mood to peace out.

Boho hippy

The original boho, this girl channels her inner flower child in loose clothing made from materials such as crochet, denim, and light linens. Keep this look contemporary boho rather than washed-hobo by introducing neon tones, digital prints, and round-lensed sunglasses.

Key accents: Smock dresses, maxi skirts, straw fedora, feather earrings, floral headpiece, denim or fur waistcoats, gladiator sandals

Make-up: Bronzer, bindi, thick brows

Hair: Wear open or braided

Muse: Kalki, Sienna Miller

Shop: Forever21, Ritu Kumar

Boho glamour

My personal favourite of the three and the most modern interpretation of bohemian dressing. This look re-imagines the glamour of the 70s, predominantly with dramatic maxi dresses in ornate colours and fabrics. Forage for vintage saris, which you can recast as dresses in classic Indian prints such as paisley. Accessories are metallic, luxurious and bold; try wearing a statement cuff above your elbow as an arm band or fashion an old earring into an original headband.

Key accents: Long-sleeved maxi dresses or vintage saris, wide brimmed floppy hats, bejewelled headpieces, raffia wedges, gold hoop earrings, statement clutch

Make-up: Shimmering bronzer, metallic eye-shadows, glossy lips

Hair: Luxuriously blow dried with flicking outwards, parted in the middle

Muse: Sonam Kapoor in Anamika Khanna

Shop: Azara by Alpana and Neeraj, Amit Aggarwal (Pernia's Pop-Up Shop), Anamkika Khanna (Pernia's Pop-Up Shop)

Boho rock-chick

More vampy than your average tambourine clanging hippy. This girl likes to combine punk and boho accents to create a harder-edged look. Black, lace, and leather is used more pervasively than in other interpretations and hemlines are much scantier.

Key items: Ripped t-shirts, denim hot pants, bowler hat, black leather fringed waistcoat, guitar.

Make-up: Nude lips, kohl eyeliner

Hair: Heavy fringe

Muse: Kate Moss, Anushka Manchanda

Shop: www.topshop.com and Rohit Gandhi and Rahul Khanna (Pernia's Pop-Up Shop)

Summer holiday fashion ideas

Winter fashion ideas

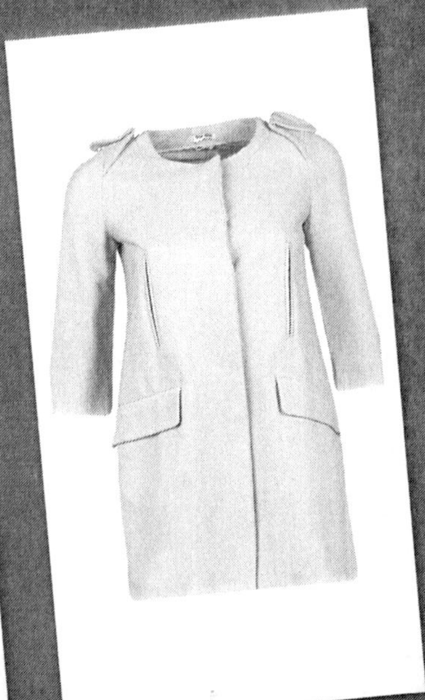

Accenting ideas

Animal print ▶

◀ *Neon*

Boho

Vintage

Leather

Boho hair to boot

One of the prettiest and simplest way to carve a hippy accent into your look is with braids and headpieces. Soft pigtails, waterfall braids, and french plaits give such an appealing, laidback dimension to any outfit.

GENERAL BOHO TIPS

- Hem lines should be either mini or maxi—nothing in between.
- Jangle your jewellery: pile on the accessories, so long as each piece is individual and comes with an amazing memory.
- Bags are soft and worn long across the body. Quirky details such as fringing or a tassel.

Vintage

We've all been there. You shimmy up to the party, meet your friends and head to the dancefloor, sassy and smug in your recently bought mini dress. Then suddenly you hear your friends gasp. It's as though the music has stopped and you're the only one left dancing. You can feel what seems like a hundred pairs of eyes boring into the back of the now lacklustre curls on your head. You look around and find, to your horror, that your gaze is met with your reflection, in an identical outfit. A kind friend offers you a tissue, another suggests you 'customize' in the washroom but you all know it's too late. Your fashion party is over.

Turning up in the same outfit as someone else is a recurring and valid style nightmare precisely because to look stylish means to look *uniquely* like you. Of course, we all shop in many of the same places, but being forced to face the reality that other women will select the same outfits *and* wear them in exactly the same way is an understandably terrifying prospect. So, how to combat the chances of running into your dreaded doppelganger? Answer: with vintage accents.

I love clothes from different eras, but it's important to be clear from the beginning what I mean by 'vintage'.

MANY PEOPLE MAKE BIG MISTAKES WHEN DRESSING BY ASSUMING THEIR LOOK CAN BE CLASSED AS VINTAGE WHEN IT REALLY JUST LOOKS OUTDATED AND SHABBY.

There is one style camp who thinks that the age of the garment denotes it's vintage. But I would preach caution in following this line of thought. You're still at high risk of looking like you're dressed in charitable donations, even if the item is practically an antique. Similarly, there are many beautiful pieces from the 80s, 90s and even early 2000s which I would class as vintage, although their style, cut, and finish may feel contemporary.

Age ain't nothin' but a number in the game of vintage. Instead, fabric and finish is all. Just as a vintage champagne has to be of excellent quality when it's first set down, so must the vintage pieces you cherry-pick be intrinsically beautiful if they are to be enjoyed for decades to come.

Charity-shop chic?

Thrift stores, garage sales and charity shops are such fun places to shop in, and you can pick up some truly original pieces at ridiculous prices, but you do need to harness your enthusiasm in this quarter. Remember, on the whole, that they offer poorer quality second-hand items than you'll find in specialized vintage boutiques. This will serve you well on certain occasions, but beware of basing your whole look around your purchases from these places. Disguise your dirty thrift store secret by teaming it with fresh, contemporary pieces, such as a thick 80s-style cardigan with a crisp white shirt and mini skirt. Unless you're totally confident in it, don't let your thrift-store purchase dominate your outfit in the way an amazing vintage piece should be allowed to. And remember that, generally speaking, if you pile on more than one of these retro finds your look will be more old-lady-meets-bargain-bin than sophisticated spend-thrift.

How to buy vintage: what it is and when to invest

Vintage soars above second-hand clothing when the designs are iconic of a particular era, without compromising on the quality or fit of the garment. Look out for instantly recognizable pieces of indisputable elegance from the rich tapestry of fashion history; I love flapper dresses from the 20s, those flirtatious 50s prom dresses as well as the dramatic maxi dresses which were synonymous with 70s style. I always swoon at the fabrics you find in fine vintage clothing because of how luxurious the materials people used to wear. Take my grandmother for example—she wore dupattas made from real silver thread! Now that's my kind of investment piece.

Silks and cottons will last for ages and continue to wear beautifully, so look out for these while you're browsing. Colour fading is not always obvious, especially in dingy shops, so always hold your chosen piece up to the light before you buy to ensure nothing has been bleached or spoilt. Lastly, check for construction clues as signs of quality which have withstood the sands of time: boned bodices, hand sewing, flat lining, bound buttonholes, handset zippers, covered buttons, piped seams, bias-bound edges, bound seam allowances, silk linings—these are all telltale signs of quality construction in any era.

IF THE PIECE IS IN GOOD SHAPE, YOU'LL BE DULY REWARDED—I OFTEN FIND THAT THE CRAFTSMANSHIP ON VINTAGE PIECES IS MUCH MORE ATTENTIVE AND ARTFUL THAN THE DETAILING YOU'LL FIND ON SIMILAR PRICED ITEMS TODAY.

It's always wise to invest in famous pieces, like a Le Smoking, from a known fashion house, a Dior evening gown, or a classic Chanel suit. But also look out for iconic pieces from a definitive or unusual period in a designer's career, such as Alexander McQueen for Givenchy. If you don't recognize the designer, then check and research the label to find out about the garment's history and where it was made. There are some great websites which will help you date and place your item, and which will give you a good indication of its potential value.

Remember that, as with any work of art, the value of a fine vintage piece will fluctuate over time—many established labels such as Balmain, Alaïa, and Lanvin already make for sound vintage investments (with careful wearing) whose value is only set to grow.

VINTAGE ADVICE

- **Don't buy damaged goods**: Missing beads, buttons, belts, and liners are generally irreplaceable. Don't be a label snob. Buy what you can wear and makes you feel good, regardless of where it came from. If a high-value piece has been attributed to a designer, make sure it is labelled or has a concrete provenance.

- **Size matters**: Vintage clothes always come up small, so don't be depressed if you find yourself bulging at the seams of your usual size. Alterations can be expensive and sometimes impossible given the garment, so don't simply buy large in the hope of taking it in unless you've tried it on and studied its design carefully. If you're shopping online, pay careful attention to the exact dimensions of the piece to ensure it matches your vital statistics. In general, the fabric is unlikely to give as easily so you may want to allow yourself an extra half-inch to ensure it fits well.

- **Timelessness**: If you want to wear your vintage investment immediately, make sure it's something which references the current style-climate and is *wearable now.* Take jumpsuits as an example, they're all over regular stores and are a near-permanent feature of vintage boutiques. Opt for a genuine 70s original and you'll ooze a unique, Studio 54 glamour.

- **Don't be afraid of nostalgia!** The fashion world has been dominated in recent years by television series such as *Mad Men* and films like *The Great Gatsby*, so follow suit and keep your mind permeable to the cultural influences around you. Watch classic films and flick through old magazines for inspiration.
- **Keep an open mind:** It can be easy to be dismissive of the countless, slightly musty smelling items on the rails before you—but get creative with what you see. Don't instantly reject an item on account of its print or cut.
- **Avoid faux vintage:** Certain brands have tried to capitalize on our hunger for vintage chic by creating a range of slogan t-shirts in bleached or faded wash outs. Steer clear, unless it's the real deal of course.

Which decade works best for you and your body?

The wonderful thing about vintage clothes is that they were made for real women—not supermodel waifs! One of the things that women love most about vintage dressing is how flattering the cuts and fabrics can be on a feminine frame. But that's not to say that every decade will suit your individual personality. It's important to understand each era, and to ensure that it is aligned to your contemporary wardrobe today.

Once you're comfortable with the style of a certain decade, and you're sure it matches your overall aesthetic then you can begin to channel certain iconic accents from that period into your everyday wardrobe.

TIP: Vintage saris are one of the easiest ways to bask in the sumptuous originality of vintage clothes without stepping too far out of your comfort zone. I love to wear heritage blouses with digital print saris for a beautifully contrasting look.

As with all style accents—only incorporate *one* or *two* into your look. If you're making a bold statement with a 50s prom dress or 80s mini skirt, keep the make-up contemporary. This will add an interesting dimension to your outfit without running the risk of looking like you stepped out via the dress-up box.

1920s

Body shape: Tall, slim and willowy

The look: Thin silhouette lines, lots of beading and intricate work, longer length, and beautifully embellished fabrics. A little bit androgynous in some respects, so perfect for the tomboy inside you.

Icon: Daisy from *The Great Gatsby*

How to wear in your wardrobe today? Drop-waist flapper dress, modernized with a biker jacket. You can also try wearing your LBD with a feathered cape, multiple strings of pearls, or an embellished headband

1930s and 1940s

Body shape: Hourglass and pear-shaped, or big-busted girls

The look: Victory roll hair, tailored trousers, pussy-bow blouses, belted coats, brightly coloured short-sleeved tea-dresses.

Icon: Lucille Ball

How to wear in your wardrobe today? Embrace tailored trousers as if they've just arrived on your fashion radar and tuck in your favourite feminine blouse. There is no shortage of 30–40s style tea-dresses in the market, make sure you buy something belted to accentuate your waist. How ladylike!

1950s

Body shape: Hourglass and pear-shaped, or big-busted girls

The look: Red lipstick, floral sundresses, full skirts, fitted bodices, prom dresses, bolero tops, halter neck dresses, pretty cardigans, Capri length trousers. Perfectly feminine and flattering.

Icon: Madhu Bala, Betty Draper in *Mad Men*

How to wear in your wardrobe today? Tuck a white t-shirt into a full skirt and team with plimsolls and cat-eye sunglasses for a contemporary but feminine 50s look

1960s

Body shape: Long legged, androgynous, apple frames

The look: Kohl eyeliner, mini skirts, shift dresses, kaleidoscope colours such as pink and orange as well as the monochrome palate, knee high boots—indulge your inner factory girl!

Icon: Sharmilla Tagore, Twiggy

How to wear in your wardrobe today? This look can be cheaply overdone, so take care. A mini skirt worn with knee-high boots is a great way to reference the decade, as well as reworking the classic shift dress in a pop-tastic colour.

1970s

Body shape: Pear, hourglass, triangle (though bigger busted women should take caution with frilly blouses)

The look: Boho hair, crazy prints, cheesecloth blouses, bell-bottomed trousers, boho accessories, maxi dresses and caped sleeves

Icon: Zeenat Aman, Diane Von Furstenberg

How to wear in your wardrobe today? High-waisted, flared jeans with a tucked-in blouse and square shades can be a great way to channel this decade. Maxi dresses are also a fail-safe option, but go easy on the psychedelic prints.

1980s

Body shape: Petite, hourglass (though go easy on shoulder pads)

The look: Shoulder pads in everything, underwear worn as outerwear, ra-ra mini skirts, oversized slogan t-shirts with leggings, leg warmers(!)

Icon: Shri Devi, Rekha, Madonna

How to wear in your wardrobe today? Copy that wonderful power-brow of Rekha to inject a dose of 80s into your look. A black slip dress teamed with a blazer and booties will artfully reference the underwear-on-outside 80s trend.

Channel this decade's penchant for neon and wear bright, oversized slogan t-shirts—they'll look super-cute with all your jeans, leggings, and mini skirts.

WHERE TO BUY?

Ssssh...you mustn't tell her, but 80 percent of the vintage I own is my Mom's. There's a particular Valentino chiffon black mini skirt of hers, which always seems to win me compliments and that I just adore wearing. I love to think that my Mom and I have partied in the same pieces!

Good vintage boutiques can be hard to come across in India, so I suggest that you start building your collection at home by raiding your mum's closet. The chances are that whatever worked on her will look sensational on you too!

Once you've rinsed your home collection then check some of these places out....

India

- Le Mill, Mumbai (for amazing vintage inspired sunglasses)
- The Vintage Garden, Mumbai (also specializes in vintage-inspired home decor)
- Lovebirds, Delhi
- House of Blondie, Delhi

Online

- eBay (check out sellers: American vintage, great lake outfitters and American Archive)
- Vagabondnyc.com
- www.coutureallure.com

New York

- Reformation
- Beacon's Closet
- Hell's Kitchen flea market

London

- Absolute Vintage
- Portobello Road market
- Beyond Retro
- Kerry Taylor Auctions
- YMCA Boutique, King's Road
- Liberty

PERNIA'S LITTLE BLACK BOOK OF STORES

We all have one, a private listing of our deepest desires, most treasured memories and guiltiest indulgences...

My little black book is a memoir of my lifelong addiction to style. Throughout my career as a serial shopper, stylist and businesswoman, I've been fortunate to travel the world and savvy enough to scribble down the details of every stylish store I encounter.

Great style doesn't grow on trees or spring miraculously from the ground—it's devotedly curated and sold by some of the smartest and most groundbreaking retailers on the planet. These guys are working around the clock to provide you with these stunning sartorial nuggets, so it's really only polite that you swing by and take a look.

Of course, you don't always have to buy, but glean these places for stylish inspiration. Eyeball the other customers, inhale the rails of cherry-picked garments, and nourish yourself by the cabinets of accessories.

Then nip to Zara if necessary.

Delhi

Anokhi: This store is distinguished by its prints and sense of designs, and range of colours and product quality.
32 Khan Market, New Delhi

Dang: Another Hauz Khas boutique which sells glorious, contemporary jewellery at heart-thudding prices. Look out for the message in a bottle necklaces, which allows you to scribe your own message on parchment. Swoon.
24/2 Hauz Khas Village, New Delhi

En Inde: A beautiful retail space offering contemporary Indian jewellery as well as remodelled classical pieces
125/126 Meherchand Market, 1st Floor, New Delhi

Good Earth: You'll find beautifully designed, unique home and personal care products.
9 ABC, Khan Market, New Delhi

House of Blondie: Head here for some great condition vintage pieces at affordable prices. The sunglasses and wallets on sale here are pretty irresistible.
24/4 Hauz Khas Village, New Delhi

Les Parisiennes: A vintage boudoir, a unique concept store offering carefully selected womenswear, menswear, a lovely children corner and home accessories.
5B Shahpur Jat, Dada Jungi House, New Delhi

Nappa Dori: Suitcases crafted from buttery leather, embossed laptop cases and quirky toiletry bags. Truly stylish women must travel in luxury. For all your needs head to Nappa Dori.
25 Meherchand Market Lodhi Road, New Delhi

Playclan: This store combines fashion, art and design to create collections in home, apparel, gifts and stationery, inspired by vibrant colors and local culture.
Shop no. 17, Meherchand Market, Lodhi Road, New Delhi

Sarojini Nagar Market: Don't be alarmed by the crowds and hawkers; this market houses some extraordinarily stylish finds at impossibly discounted prices. Take care when rummaging through the piles of export surplus as some pieces are faulty. Otherwise, revel in the refreshingly cheap and exciting garments. The best time to visit is Friday morning.

Second Floor Studio: A concept store with an explosion of eclectic collections.
417 Shahpur Jat, Near Dada Jungi House, New Delhi

Mumbai

Bungalow 8: I always find that this shop is teaming with quirky interior pieces and exciting fashion finds. A visit will

produce an unavoidable attack of lifestyle envy so try your best not to get carried away.
Near Radio Club, Opposite Basilico Cafe, Grants Building, 1st, 2nd & 3rd floors, 17, Apollo Bunder Road, Mumbai

Bombay Electric: Colaba emporium fusing fashion and art—look out for the exceptional jewellery collections and cutest clothes for stylish kids.
1 Reay House, Best Marg, Colaba, Mumbai

Curio Cottage: India's premier jewellery store offering a perfect mix of feminine & ethnic jewellery designs.
19, Mahakavi Bhushan Marg, Behind Regal Cinema, Colaba, Mumbai

Le Mill: A former rice mill where clothes, furnishing and flowers collide into one extraordinary retail experience. This concept store is an essential pilgrimage for any stylish woman.
17-25 Nandlal Jani Road, Next to new railway bridge, Wadi Bunder, Mumbai

Sabya by Sabyasachi: Traditional India couture created by one of the finest designers in the business.

Kolkata

85 Lansdowne: Kolkata's coolest retail destination—showcasing over 45 designers from across the country.
Sarat Bose Rd, Kalighat, Kolkata

Byloom: A panoply of colours and treats await you in this renovated mansion, I love its traditional handlooms with a modern twist.
58, Hindustan Park, Gariahat, Kolkata

Junk A jewellery: Head here for jaw-dropping handcrafted jewellery. I use these exclusive pieces to ensure my outfits stay unique.
62/64 H P Dutta Lane, Kolkata

Jaipur

Amrapali: The ultimate destination for your fine jewellery fix.
Panch Batti, M I Road Jaipur

Idli Designs: Satin cocktail dresses, quilted jackets, tie-dye tunics and sexy jersey silk dresses are sold here, all crafted using traditional Indian techniques. Don't miss the eye-popping interior pieces!
C-58 B, Mahaveer Marg, C-Scheme

Nidhi Tholia: I gasp whenever I visit this designer's spacious Jaipur store. Tholia is famed for her lehengas, salwar and churidar suits, but check out her saris too, which feature traditional Gota work.
C 72 Sarojini Marg, C-Scheme, Jaipur

Ahmedabad

Elan
Monsoon
Nautanky

Hyderabad

Anahita
Anonym
Elahe

Online

- Perniaspopupshop.com (make it your homepage!)
- eBay: check out sellers like American vintage, great_lake_outfitters, and American Archive
- Netaporter.com

Paris

Colette
Corto Moldeo
Didier Ludot
L' Eclareur Fashion
Mona

New York

Barneys
Intermix
Jeffrey
Opening Ceremony
Reformation
Theory

London

Absolute Vintage
Beyond Retro
Browns
Dover Street Market
Liberty
Topshop, 216 Oxford Street, London

ACKNOWLEDGEMENTS

Firstly, I would like to thank my mom, for always inspiring me and showing me the way.

My dad and my sister for being the best support system one could ever have.

A big thank you to Sonam for her lovely words about the book.

My team—Arjun Sahwney, Prabhakar Shastry and Bhavini Modi—for helping me put this book together.

Thank you Philly Malicka for helping me with the writing.

And Trisha, from Random House India.

A NOTE ON THE AUTHOR

Pernia Qureshi, leading stylist and fashion icon, has embarked on an exciting journey in the fashion industry. With her e-commerce venture, www.perniaspopupshop.com, India's premier designers are now accessible to a global clientele.

Pernia's Pop-Up Shop is a carefully curated design platform that articulates Pernia's personal style and her accumulated experience. With this expertise at the helm, she brings you the opportunity to enhance your wardrobe with the creative excellence of our most coveted designers as well as the vibrant energy of bright young talent.